Reg

Name _____

Address _____

City _____ State____ Zip_____

Phone Number (____) _____

Type of Bus, (if any) _____

Please fill out and send to:

WINLOCK publishing company
26135 Murrieta Road
Sun City, CA 92585
(909)943-4945

    This registration will entitle you to one free update mailed to your address. You may call the above number to determine if a revision has been developed in your area of interest. In addition, you are entitled to one phone call to the author of approximately 15 minutes duration. Additional telephone consultations will be charged at the rate of $100 per hour billed in 15 minute increments.
    Except for FAX, this phone will be answered only between 9:00 AM and 4:00 PM Pacific Time. If you get an answer machine with no reply, we are on the road. We'll get back to you.
    WINLOCK publishing is devoted exclusively to publishing bus and conversion information, along with computer generated bus data. By registering, you will also be notified of new products and books.

The Bus Converter's Bible

How to Plan and Create Your Own Luxury Motorhome

Dave Galey
B. S. Architectural Engineering

WINLOCK publishing company
Sun City, California

The Bus Converter's Bible
How to Plan and Create Your Own Luxury Motorhome

by Dave Galey
B.S. Architectural Engineering

Published by:
WINLOCK publishing company
26135 Murrieta Road
Sun City, California 92585

All rights reserved. No part of this book may be reproduced or transmitted by any form or by any means, electronic, or mechanical, including photocopying, recording or by any information storage and retrieval system without written permission from the author, except for the inclusion of a brief quotation in a review.

Copyright © 1995 by Dave Galey

Library of Congress Cataloging-in-Publication Data
Galey, Dave
 The bus converter's manual: how to plan and create your own luxury motorhome / by Dave Galey
 Library of Congress Catalog Number: 95-62089

ISBN 0-9649437-4-3 : $49.95

Unless otherwise credited, all photographs and drawings are by the author.
Page 17, drawing from Eagle Parts Book
Page 112, photograph courtesy Fred Space
Page 157, photograph courtesy Marvin Zepede
Typesetting and cover design by the Author

Table of Contents

Preface 9
Introduction 13
Part One   **Structural Modifications** 17
1   Getting Started 19
2   Raising the Roof 23
3   Stretching Exercises 29
4   Other Structural Modifications 33
5   Extendable Floor Space 37
6   Side Hinged Baggage Doors 43
7   The Steel Case 51
8   Swing-Out Radiator (Eagle) 59
9   Hinged Utility Support Structure 65
Part Two   **Plumbing** 69
10   Introduction to Plumbing 71
11   Materials 73
12   Fresh Water Tankage 77
13   Fittings and Equipment 83
14   Fixtures 89
15   Waste Water Schematic 95
16   Black Water Scheme 97
17   Grey Water Scheme 99
18   Piping and Fittings 103
19   Liquid Petroleum Gas 107
Part Three   **Electrical Systems** 113
20   Power Requirements 115
21   Battery Requirements 119
22   Generators 123
23   Converters, Inverters, and Chargers 129
24   Fittings and Material 133
25   Electrical Circuits....................... 139

26	Electronic Systems and Circuits	149
27	Gauges and Instrumentation	153
Part Four	**Heating and Air Conditioning**	157
28	Basic Considerations	159
29	Heating and Air Conditioning Basics	163
30	Heating	179
31	Ventilation	195
32	Air Conditioning	199
33	Summary: Heating and Air Conditioning	213
Part Five	**Interior Design**	217
34	Floor Plans	219
35	Walls and Bulkheads	225
36	Headliners	229
37	Window Dressing	233
38	Cabinets	237
39	Floor Treatment	241
Part Six	**Exterior Design**	243
40	Body Work	245
41	Prime Coats	249
42	Graphics and Paint Systems	253
43	Engines and Transmissions	259
44	Tires and Suspensions	263
Conclusions		267
Appendix		269
Index		279
Re-order Form		286,288

About the Author

Dave Galey has an engineering degree from the University of Oklahoma, 1952. He spent twenty years as an aircraft structural designer. He did research work in honeycomb sandwich structure, and prepared a design manual while in the aircraft business. While there, he developed reinforced plastic products for the oil industry.

With Hunter Engineering, he designed aluminum processing equipment and later left engineering to become a retail merchant. As a career change, in partnership with his brother, he became an oil producer. This business was recently sold.

He fell in love with buses about 15 years ago, and converted his first bus then. As a hobby, he has worked on many of his friends buses, and has converted several buses for others. He completed his latest personal coach a little over six years ago.

Dave, with his wife Roberta have traveled extensively throughout the United States, Canada and Mexico in their conversions. As a hobby, Dave continues to upgrade his computer, so that he may write articles and illustrate them with engineering drawings. In addition, Dave has analyzed the structure of buses. When it comes to structural modifications, such as slide-out rooms. He and his friends have developed several innovations. He and his wife have six children and thirteen grandchildren.

Warning-Disclaimer

This book is designed to provide information only on the subject matter covered. It is sold with the understanding that the publisher and author are not engaged in rendering legal, accounting, engineering, or other professional services. If legal or other expert assistance is required, the services of a competent professional should be sought.

It is not the purpose of this manual to reprint all the information otherwise available to the author and/or publisher, but to complement, amplify and supplement other texts. You are urged to read all the available material, learn as much as possible about bus conversion and to tailor the information to your individual needs.

Every effort has been made to make this manual as complete and as accurate as possible. However, there may be mistakes both typographical and in content. Therefore, this text should be used only as a general guide and not as the ultimate source of bus conversion. Furthermore, this manual contains information on bus conversion only up to the printing date.

The purpose of this manual is to educate and entertain. The author and **WINLOCK publishing company** shall have neither liability nor responsibility to any person or entity with respect to any loss or damage caused, or alleged to be caused, directly or indirectly by the information contained in this book.

If you do not wish to be bound by the above, you may return this book to the publisher for a full refund.

Preface

This book is written for those hearty souls desiring to own and enjoy a large, one of a kind, mobile suite of rooms, able to transport them and their family to the places of their dreams, and provide them with all the comforts of home. Moreover, it is designed to supply much information that will enable the individual to select various approaches, choose materials and configurations to fabricate, or have made for them, those features they believe will enhance their pleasure and use of this vehicle.

The material contained in this book is an accumulation of ideas developed over a fifteen year love affair with buses, and the satisfaction of seeing these, and ideas of my friends, turned into functional hardware. I make no apology for lifting ideas from other innovators. Having received my degree in engineering from a national leader in collegiate football over forty years ago, and with the intervening experience, one thing I have learned is that I have no monopoly on creative thoughts. In fact, I seem to have a talent for picking up on the ideas of others, and converting them to practicality.

Most of my background was spent as a designer for a couple of major airframe manufacturers. I went through a love affair with sailing for a decade and a half, then the next decade of recreation was devoted to flying, during which I became an instrument rated pilot. I found both sailing and flying were limited, in that you could visit many marinas, or landing strips, but not much more. So, I descended from these lofty pursuits to become an earth-bound bus driver. In these past fifteen years, my bride and I have traveled, in the company of a unique class of individuals, the depths of Mexico, the magnificence of the United States, and parts of Canada, totalling in all, over 150,000 miles.

In these experiences we have made mistakes, and hope we have learned from them. In that time I have converted two coaches for ourselves, and have helped many friends convert their buses. Many times, I have been tempted to go into the business of conversion, since its popularity has grown immensely over the years, but I remember the demands of being in business, its set backs and disappointments. Moreover, we cherish our freedom from obligations; our ability to pick up and leave when we want. And, if I get an overwhelming desire to put something down on paper (or video screen) my trusty computer is never very far away.

A few individuals must be mentioned that have influenced my busing. Bob Howell, sometimes known as the

Preface

Father of the Eagle Conversion, is foremost not only for his uniqueness, but his friendship. Jack Headley, former skipper of the Wild Goose, John Wayne's private yacht, must be singled out for his innovative ideas and wry sense of humor.

Mention must be made of Mike Kadletz, publisher of *Bus Conversion* magazine, and Larry Cronkite, its first editor, who were kind enough to include me as one of their writers.

Larry Plachno, editor and publisher of the *National Bus Trader*, a hard task master, has my gratitude for his inspiration and for motivating me to actually put this book together. Although Larry and I don't always agree how to write about a subject, his professionalism is greatly admired.

Dick Wright, a close and personal friend, probably knows more about busing than most people you'll ever meet. Dick is always ready to help a novice. Then there are the many, many friends who allowed me to experiment on their coaches, Phil Barger, Bill Young, Jerry Liotta, Jerry Averhart, and too many others to mention. George Thornhill, the expert on the venerable old GM4104, must be acknowledged for his incisive mind and his desire to teach. Harold "Ike" Eickmeyer, an electronic talent and *full timer*, has my gratitude for his ideas and his friendship. Morrie Maxwell of Bakersfield (my favorite breakdown spot), is always ready to help out. Thanks to "*ZIP*" Zepede for a great idea, and to Russell Davies of Mapleton, Utah, a real talent.

Most important, my gratitude to my loving and patient co-pilot, Roberta, who agreed to proof read this manuscript and take the blame for all technical and typographic errors. After all, isn't that what wives are for? I would like to thank Dick Wright, George Phillips, Dale DeWitt, Suzie McDonell and Jack Filion who served as a peer review board, calling gross errors, both technical and grammatical, to my attention.

Finally, my thanks and gratitude to my editor, Fran Jessee.

Keep in mind, while going through this book, the ideas presented here are just that, ideas. No claim is made that any idea is better than the next. The designs presented are one way of solving a problem. This is not to say they are the only way to do it. If there were only one answer to an engineering problem, no doubt, we would only have one bus shell, or one automobile instead of many to choose from. Most of the actual designs and fabricated ideas discussed in this book are centered around the Eagle coach. Although, I have worked on MCIs, GMs, Prevosts, and Flxibles, the Eagle offers an exceptional versatility for innovations. For those of you involved with other coaches (OBs, that is, *other brands*), the concepts are the same, only the structural details may be more complex.

Putting this book together has been a labor of love. I hope it is a beginning, and that the readers who are critical of some of the things in this book will contact the publisher and let their ideas be known. In this manner, the content will continually be improved with subsequent printings.

ENJOY THE BOOK!

Dave Galey
Fall 1995

I herewith dedicate this book
to my
loving copilot:

Roberta

Introduction

Because of the explosive popularity of the recreational vehicle, and the luxurious treatment seen in today's motorhomes, the intercity bus has become a logical choice for the individual converter to direct their energies. By this, I mean the brave soul, unable to afford a professional conversion, attacking the problem head-on.

I have seen bus conversions attending rallies with nothing more than an air mattress, a porta-potty, and a camp stove, while its owner is in the process of converting it into a rolling luxury suite. It has been fascinating to see the metamorphic change as these sow's ears turn into silk purses. The variations are limited only by the imagination of the craftsman doing the work. Moreover, the owner will develop skills he didn't earlier possess.

The most popular coaches for conversions are the venerable GM4104, GM4106, The Flxible VL-100, the Oh-one Eagle, the Oh-five Eagle, the MCI-5, the MCI-7,-8, and -9. I have purposely omitted the newer coaches such as the Prevosts, the model 15 Eagles, the Neoplans, and the MCI A102s. These bare bus shells are quite expensive. If you have the capability of affording these newer coaches, you can probably afford to have a professional conversion company do the job for you. On the other hand, if you are the type who takes pride in doing a certain job and can afford these newer coaches, good luck and thank you for buying this book.

What will a bus shell cost, and where can it be obtained? This can vary on the low side of a few thousand dollars, upward to nearly three-hundred thousand dollars. Buses are continuously being replaced by charter coach companies, and of course there are the big re-sellers such as Hausman and ABC bus. Look in the *National Bus Trader*, and *Bus Conversions* Magazine. These magazines advertise coaches for sale every month. You may also look in the *FMCA* magazine and *Motorhome* magazine classified section.

A word about the binding of this book is in order. Since it is possible, and hoped that this book will be used in a shop environment, the cover is protected with a plastic laminate, and the binding is assembled with a lay-flat glue. This simply means that you may lay the book open, smooth it out, and it will stay that way, like a shop manual. In addition, this may be done repeatedly without the book falling apart, so I have been assured.

At the beginning of some chapters you will find a space for notes and an area to make sketches. This will permit you to personalize this book, as you plan your conversion. It is suggested you include this personalized edition with your important bus papers, for future reference.

One other suggestion about this book. This book is *not* designed to be read like a novel. Jump around. Look for the subject which interests you at the time. Since it is designed to be used as reference material, occasionally you will find subjects repeated so you will be sure to get the message. Some of the topics covered will not interest everybody, but there is something for all.

One cautionary comment I wish to stress is safety. Every state has its own rules about motor vehicle safety. In addition, most states have regulations concerning the combining of a motor vehicle with living quarters, hence a mobilehome, or a motorhome. For example, in the state of California, the Department of Housing and Community Development, Division of codes and Standards is a regulatory agency that will, for a fee, inspect your coach, leave you a pamphlet with the rules to follow. They will then re-inspect your vehicle for compliance and issue you an RVIA decal.

If you wish to obtain a copy of these standards write to National Fire Protection Association, Batterymarch Park, Quincy, MA 02269, or Recreational Vehicle Industry Association, 1896 Preston White Drive, Reston, VA 22090. Ask for Bulletin ANSI A119.2/NFPA 501C, Recreational Vehicles Edition. This is a 38 page booklet which is tantamount to the Uniform Building Code for the RV

Introduction

industry.

By following this code, you will not only provide for your own safety, but also your subsequent buyer, assuming you can part with your labor of love. And, as a seller you assume a level of liability with your buyer. An approval from your state safety agency and this decal will go a long way to mitigate this liability.

A number of years ago, before the RVIA became recognized, it was suggested that when you sold your conversion to issue a bill of sale reading "*An unfinished housecar*," regardless of the level of completion. This admonishment put the buyer on notice they were not buying anything but a home built conversion. Although this may still be done, be safe; check with your state's safety agency and comply with all the requirements.

This book will take the reader through the concepts for structural modifications. Many of the ideas are unique, and all of them have been done with success. Many of the structural alterations have been applied to the Eagle, but virtually all coaches have a similar design philosophy. Elevating the roof of a coach, regardless of its make, will simply increase its bending stiffness and torsional resistance, within limits. **This, of course, demands equal or greater skin and structure be used**. Many of the chapters in this section have appeared, in some form, in earlier *Bus Conversion* magazine issues.

I cannot emphasize too strongly structural modifications without a working knowledge of stresses and strains, or a close acquaintance with an engineer who can assist, may lead a person into problems. So, be very cautious when making any radical changes. Keep in mind much of the skin of the MCI series is also working to keep the bus together, that is, stressed skin.

Sections on Plumbing and Electrical are really quite common to residential or earthbound buildings. Of course, there are some things unique to the motorhome such as carrying your water and waste with you, that are normally taken care of by the public utilities. The electrical section also includes both alternating and direct current, along with the instructions to size your anticipated loads.

Heating and Air Conditioning are unique to the motorhome concept, except that the basic laws of physics still prevail. That is, heat loss and heat loads are still subject to insulation factors, and configuration.

A small treatment on interior design is included but will not train you to become a bus architect. Nor will the section on exterior design teach you to become a body and fender man, a graphic artist or an automotive painter. These sections are included so you might discuss various approaches with any professional you might decide to employ.

Finally, under exterior design, I have included some thoughts on the primary power plant, your engine. I discuss some of the options on re-powering, and some of the things to avoid.

The thoughts here are my own, and not all the experts will agree with me. But, after all, this is what bus converting is all about,--------- **DOING IT YOUR WAY ! !**

Part One

Structural Modifications

Chapter One

Getting Started

So, you bought a bus shell and finally have it home. It's huge. Where do you start? You have been scheming for months but are just a little bit bewildered. One smart thing you did was to make a deal with the seller to discount the selling price by removing and keeping the passenger seats. Now its your turn to get started.

One tool which is a "must" is one of those **impact screw drivers**. Unless you had a lot of bucks to spend, chances are that the coach you bought will be a few years old and will be loaded with old fashioned slotted head screws. Although many of these screws will be stainless steel, they will be fastened into aluminum, or mild steel and be thoroughly corroded in place, hence the impact screw driver. Another *must have* tool is a battery operated drill with screw driver bits, both Phillips and slotted.

Your first task is to clean out the interior. The first challenge is to remove the overhead baggage racks. Often this can be done in sections. Other times it must be removed in one piece unless you have a method of sawing it apart. It will be useful to have a friendly neighbor, or invite some pals over to admire, inspect, and heckle your folly. Be sure and provide appropriate liquid refreshment. The next step is to tackle the toilet. These are ingeniously installed and sometimes you wonder just what the installation sequence was during the initial construction of your coach. The whole procedure is like working a jigsaw puzzle in reverse. Then continue by removing the inside walls and ceiling, and finally the insulation. If you are stripping an MCI, a word of caution is required ; the inside aluminum skin must be left in tact, since it is load bearing, that is, stresses skin. Leave it in place,

The Bus Converter's Bible

or plan to replace it. Scrap the insulation and plan to install new material. Most of the older coaches used fiberglass, which over the years tends to lose some of its effectiveness.

Much of the scrap aluminum you remove has a salvage value, so plan to sell it to a scrap yard. Scrap aluminum prices have fluctuated from 20 to 80 cents per pound for clean extrusion. If it has any screws or steel in it, it will be significantly discounted. Decide if it is worth your time to clean it up. Most of the fasteners are junk, even the stainless steel screws. And, all of the wood or plastic should be relegated to the dumpster.

Most of the wiring in the overhead may be stripped, since most of it was used for passenger service. The ICC marker lights may be re-wired, or the old wire may be left in. This circuit is very simple, so it presents no problems for the novice. In chapter Twenty Five, circuits are discussed with a diagram for completely replacing the automotive wiring if this is desired.

You now have a fine looking tunnel. You are able to see the

Getting Started

inside of all the outside skin, and can trace all the marker light wiring. The next step depends on what your ultimate plans are. Do you plan to re-side the bus completely? Are you going to raise the roof for additional headroom? Maybe you like it the way it is, and are ready to start building your interior. If this is true, you still have a few decision to make. Do you want to keep the coach air conditioning ? If you do, you will have to sacrifice some baggage capacity along with engine power needed to run the compressor and the blowers, and it will only be useful while you are under way. This can be a big plus (see the section on Air Conditioning). If you have decided to do away with the coach A/C, you now have a project on your hands. Again, it is like a reverse jigsaw puzzle. Some of those double wall A/C ducts under the floor can drive you to drink as you remove them.

    Remove anything in the baggage compartment that is no longer needed. These items may be such things as the bus passenger heating core along with the blowers and motors, which occupies a significant amount of space, and the air conditioning pump and condenser. Also, remove unneeded linkage and control rods in the tunnel or floor chase. For example, if you plan to install an automatic transmission, it may be controlled by a Morse type cable, so the old shift linkage is no longer necessary. An air throttle, or cable throttle control will replace the old throttle linkage, so take it out.

    What condition is the floor? I've seen floors in buses that are in great shape, but often some coaches show a little dry rot near the entry door, and especially in the vicinity of the toilet. For the cost of eight, or ten sheets of exterior A-C plywood, you are better off to replace the floor. Again, remove any insulation below the floor and plan to replace it. Many coaches have a form of spongy linoleum over the floor, and often some of it is cracked or broken. So, replace it all. The advantage of removing all the original floor is that you may now inspect all the structure and satisfy yourself that it is sound, and if it is not, it may be replaced as necessary. The first non-destructive task is to install a new floor of plywood. This should be a minimum of ¾ inch. Tongue and groove is recommended. Tec screws (screws with self drilling points) are suggested, but #6 drywall screws are acceptable by pre-drilling a 1/8-inch diameter hole.

 Now that you have a clean floor to work on, decide whether you wish to keep the original bus windows. Most of us replace the bus windows with sliding glass windows and screens. These are available from several companies such as Hehr, Kinro and Peninsula. Many RV dealers can supply them, or you can buy direct in many cases. The next job is to remove the bus windows where you want plain walls. One comment: the less windows you have the more efficient your heating and cooling is, but you must balance a workable floor plan and your level of claustrophobia. Do you plan to raise the roof ? That is the subject of a future chapter. The window openings that are to be blanked-out may be covered with aluminum, steel sheet or whatever suits your fancy (see the chapter, The Steel Case) .

 You have only one task left to complete the "getting started" phase. Tape your floor plan on your nice clean plywood floor with 3/4-inch masking tape, then spray it with a can of contrasting color of paint. Then peel off the masking tape and you have a fairly permanent plan with which to work. (See Chapter Thirty Four, Floor Plans). Now ask your *significant other*, be she your wife or lover, to go into the bus and inspect the plan. Be sure to select a different contrasting color so you may re-do the plan to her satisfaction. Keep several colors on hand. Some prefer to wait until all floor planning is done to tape and spray the floor- it's your choice.

You have now started!

Chapter Two

Raising the Roof

In recent years, it has become very fashionable to raise the roof of our bus conversions. This is done for several very practical reasons. First, many people converting buses for their own use are at, or near the 75 inches of headroom required by the DOT for a public conveyances, i.e., they are over six feet tall. Also, the added height allows much more cupboard space, duct space, and wire chase space. Finally, the additional bragging rights are not to be discounted. In this chapter, it is my intention to explain a step-by-step procedure, describing how to raise the roof of a bus, single-handed, ie., no help needed! O.K.?

There are several basic requirements in order to achieve the results stated above. You must be capable of welding. . .the welds don't have to be pretty (they can look like bubble gum), but they must achieve penetration. The welds will be ground flush, so with a little luck you might pass for a certified pipeline welder. You should have or be able to borrow, an abrasive cut-off saw for steel. Finally, you'll need almost 30, three inch "C" clamps. The rest of the items can be fabricated for very little money.

From any automobile wrecking yard, you can pick up four bumper jacks for about five bucks each. With the jacks I bought, I added to their height by welding 1½-inch square tubing, so they would reach from the bus floor to the window header, and still provide for an additional eight inch, or so, extension. This extension is the amount you wish to raise your roof. At the jack pad, a short length of angle was welded to provide a uniform bearing point against the window header.

The Bus Converter's Bible

The last set of tools needed are simply some lengths of 2" by 2" by 1/4" steel angles. These will be used to clamp against the window mullions (the vertical members), to maintain t he original alignment. You should have five (5) pieces the ʰight of the window, and five (5) pieces the window heig it less the two corner radii. These shorter pieces should be able to nest inside the window opening and lay flush along the mullion. These parts will make five sets. Now, we are ready to begin.

(1) Remove all your side windows from your bus. Remove your front and rear caps or cut through them so the only thing connecting the roof to the bus body are the window mullions. Some people feel it is necessary to remove the windshields, but I have raised roofs by simply cutting along a crease line on existing caps (as shown above) without disturbing the windshields. Then, we fill the gap with fiber

Raising the Roof

glass and resin. These are choices you will have to make.

(2) Using your chop saw, cut your spacers to length. This length is the height you wish to raise the roof. These spacers will be fitted inside the window mullions after they are cut. Set up a jig so each spacer is cut to the same length. I have seen coaches raised as much as 12 inches. 6 inches has been the most popular, but lately 8 inches has grown in favor. With reference to an Eagle bus, the window mullions are 40 mm square tubing with a 3 mm wall thickness. **This material may be ordered from the Eagle factory in Texas**, or you may substitute 1½-inch square tubing with a wall thickness of 1/8-inch. This is slightly smaller than the metric tubing, but after you add the exterior skin and the interior material, the coach shell will be stiffer than the original bus.

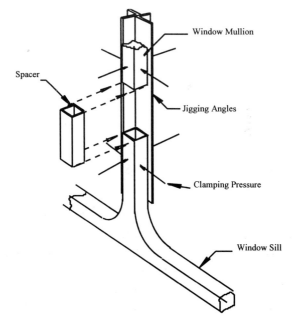

(3) Place the bumper jacks at the four corner windows along the side of the bus and clamp them to the window sill, positioning the lifting pad under the header. Apply a little jacking pressure. Using the built-in clamp of the chop saw, position it on a window mullion, so it lays horizontal. Cut through the mullion. Its vertical position is not important. What is important is that the saw is clamped perpendicular to the vertical member. This provides a square cut so that your spacers maintain alignment. Repeat this procedure until only four mullions remain intact at the corners.

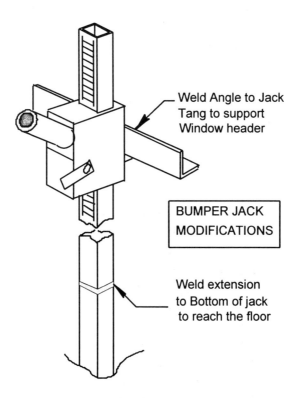

Raising the Roof

(4) **Before the final four mullions are cut, the roof must be stabilized.** At the cut mullion closest to each jack, clamp a long angle on the outside, flange forward, and extending slightly back of the member, with two clamps; one on each side of the cut. Using the short length of angle, back it up against the outside angle and clamp it to the mullion with a clamp on each side of the cut. This cross-section of angles approximate an "X", with the corners bearing against each other and the mullion nestled between them. Do this at each of the four corner windows. With the coach roof thus stabilized, you may now make your final cuts to free the bus roof from the rest of the coach.

(5) Starting at one corner, release the clamps, either above or below the cut, and jack up the roof about an inch, or so. Re-tighten the clamps, and go to the next corner. Repeat the procedure. Continue around the bus in a consistent pattern until you have reached the desired height. If you have helpers, set up a schedule where each person releases the clamps, jacks up the roof, and re-clamps in a clockwise direction. Never release more than one corner at a time.

(6) Grind a bevel on the stub ends of the cut mullions, and the spacers. This will insure adequate weld penetration. You are now ready to install your spacers.

(7) Pick a convenient point near a jack, and install a spacer. You may have to let the jack down a little. Using your fifth set of angles, jig the spacer in place; using a set of clamps above and below the spacer and on the spacer. You now have 22 clamps in use.

(8) Weld the two exposed sides of the spacer to the mullions, top and bottom. Remove one alignment angle, and make those welds. Remove the other angle and weld those seams. Continue this procedure at all the other positions.

Occasionally, you might have to use a *come-along* winch to bring the parts together.

(9) You may now remove the four stabilizing sets of alignment angles, and install those spacers. **The roof is raised!** Your final task is to grind the welds flush. Re-weld where necessary, and re-grind. Spray each area with a good primer to prevent corrosion.

The final process is to repair the old caps, or install new ones. Refer to Chapter Forty, **Body Work** for information on repairing the old caps. New caps may be installed with sealant and rivets. Avoid silicone rubber as a sealant since it does not accept body filler or paint. A superior sealant is a product of Sikaflex, or 3M. The inexpensive butyl rubber sealant available at all home improvement centers works satisfactory. It generally goes under the name of latex caulk. Even if you install new caps, a certain amount of body work is unavoidable.

Virtually all conversion companies are a source for fiberglass caps, perhaps the most prominent independent supplier is R & M Fiberglass of Turner, Oregon.

Chapter Three

Stretching Exercises

The Eagle bus. What a magnificent and versatile coach it is. For at least ten years it has been customary to raise the roof on the Eagle, and this has been done from five to ten inches in height. Many Eagles have also had the cab section raised to bring the driver's position level with the main floor, thus adding much more livable space when converted to a motorhome. Eagles have also been widened to the maximum legal width by adding one and one-half by three inch rectangular tubing to the lower section, and splicing in a six-inch spacer in the middle of the roof bows.

Now the forty-five-foot coach is all the rage. So the humble, versatile Eagle has been stretched, and is the subject of this chapter.

In 1993, an Eagle near me was lengthened. As a retired structural engineer, my involvement included some "hand waving", and looking at a few numbers. If you want to make any structural modifications to the Eagle bus, and have any questions, I have been told the Eagle plant in Brownsville, Texas will be happy to guide and advise you.

First, I would like to editorialize about this procedure: I feel it essential that only Model-One Eagles be considered for this modification. I converted my first coach about fourteen years ago, a Model-One, and drove it deep into Mexico and over most of the "forty-eight" for about eight years. Six years ago, I finished my keeper, a Model-Five, and have driven it over 60,000 miles, again deep into Mexico, and over most of the "forty-eight." It took me almost a year to get used to maneuvering the Model-Five, after wasting a couple of bogie tires and pitching the dishes out of the cupboards going around corners. In fact, one place in Mexico I had to back down six blocks since I couldn't make a turn without going through a local living room. The thing I had to learn is the Model-Five, with its wheel base lengthened 25% (that is from 20 feet to 25 feet), is not as maneuverable as the Model-One.

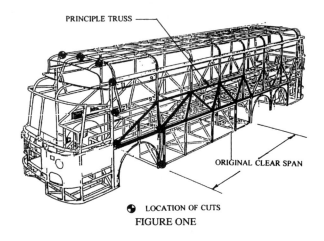

FIGURE ONE

If you will examine Figure One, the principle truss will be evident. This section spans between the rear bulkhead of the steering axle and forward bulkhead of the drive axle. The targets shown are the locations of the cuts. If the original forward roof cap sub-structure has been removed in preparation to add a model 10 cap, obviously it is not necessary to make the cuts over the roof section. The vehicle was positioned on a reasonably flat concrete slab and was braced on jack stands at each bulkhead location and under the vertical members of the baggage compartment just aft of the cuts. In this day of modern technology, it would have been nice to have used laser alignment tools but a stretched string proved to be equally as effective. The forward section was moved forward as shown in Figure Two. A backhoe was used in this case, but a forklift or even some dollies could be used since the section is not unusually heavy. The distance chosen to lengthen the coach corresponds to the length of the section between the steering axle bulkheads as shown in Figures Two and Three. This distance is approximately sixty-two inches, and increases the span between major bulkheads a little over one third. That is, from a span of one to a span of one and one-third.

By increasing the span by one-third the bending stresses are nearly doubled, and in the case of a truss structure whose stresses are simple compression and tension, the same is also true. In order to maintain structural integrity we added square tubing along the top chord and lower chord (known as doubling), of the clear span truss. This was done similar to boat building techniques by sistering new steel to the existing steel with butt welds and stitch welds. After the alignment and welding of new truss

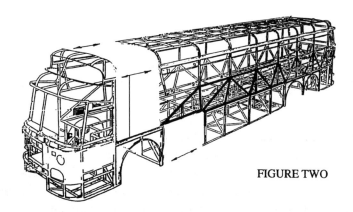

FIGURE TWO

structure in place, longerons were added where needed and the baggage compartment was filled in. A new roof frame (bow) was required and this was fabricated by bending and welding. This member may also be ordered from Eagle Coach Corporation. We

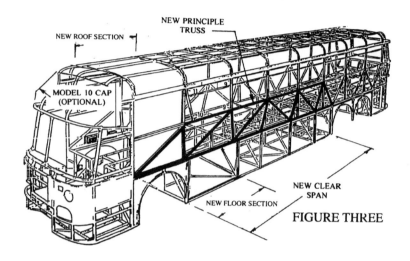

FIGURE THREE

investigated the torsional rigidity of the body and found by using tubing of equivalent size and gage, nothing additional was needed.
    If you feel compelled to stretch a Model-Five, or Ten, etc., I strongly recommend it be done in two stages. That is, add half your stretch forward of the steering axle and half, aft of the drive axle since it would not be too smart to add another five feet to the wheel base. Otherwise, you might find out that it can't be maneuvered without a steerable drive axle.

Chapter Four

Other Structural Modifications

A bus, by its very nature, is probably one of the most difficult vehicles on which to provide mechanical maintenance. Because of its passenger floor needs and its boxey shape, and the engine buried beneath all that, motor maintenance is very difficult, especially when compared to a big-rig style truck where the hood section folds over so that the mechanic may have un-obstructed access to all parts of the engine.

The Eagle coach, as it comes from the factory, has floor hatches over strategic parts of the motor, but the left-hand side of the motor is still blocked by the radiator and fan. (More about solving this problem in a later chapter). Furthermore, if *Jake Brakes* are employed, the high valve covers are very difficult to remove for tunes-ups and other engine problems.

In a coach converted to a motorhome other design considerations may also hamper access to vital parts of the coach. For example, I need to replace my fuel gauge sender, a VDO straight rigid unit 22 inches long, but the old fuel tank sender is located directly beneath my shower stall, and the tank is almost impossible to remove. What is more, due to baffling in the tank a Stewart Warner, "broken arm" sender will not function. So I use a dipstick through the filler neck to check my fuel condition.

Getting back to the *engine access solution,* for those of you planning a bed in the back, the simple thing to do is open the floor under the bed, hinge the bed platform so it may be lifted up, then you will achieve unlimited access to the top of the motor. But, what does this do to the rigidity of the bus frame in a critical area?

Imagine a bread box with a hole out of the side or top of it. Its resistance to twisting has been severely compromised. The most twist resistant structural form is a tube or pipe. The torsional resistance of a rectangular box is no more than the resistance of a tube which may be fitted inside that box.

But access holes, hatches and doors are cut out of all forms of vehicles. So there certainly is a way to do it without compromising the performance and integrity of the structure. This is traditionally done by ridgidizing the structure around the opening, commonly called doubling, or adding doublers.

Doublers may take almost any form. Around an outside section of stressed skin, for example, if it is reasonably small

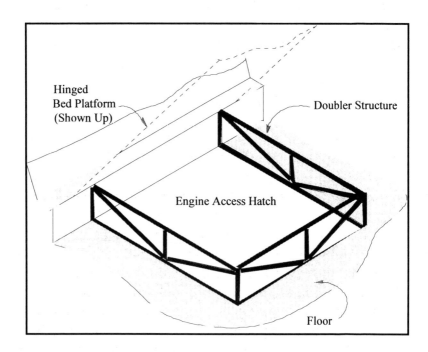

such as a hand access hatch, it is common to simply add another thickness of skin, which is also used as a door jamb for the access port. In a large opening, such as a cargo door, the doubler may take the shape of a ridged frame of some huskiness.

Getting back to our access hatch over the engine and under the bed, the simplest solution is to build up steel beams vertically surrounding the opening, and use them to support the bed platform, as shown in the illustration. The beams in question are fabricated with diagonal web members, but can be just as effective with sheet metal skin filling between the top and bottom members.

If single beds are planned for each side of the coach, hatches may be installed beneath them, but they don't need as much reinforcing as one large hatch. It is possible the existing hatches are quite serviceable with a twin bed design. However, a central hatch should be included in the aisle.

Other Structural Modifications

How significant is six inches? Not very much when you are considering the overall length of a coach, but consider it added to the width and it takes on a completely new significance. I recall when the 102-wide Prevosts came on the scene, and a female friend of mine was asked," What good is another six inches?" Her reply was, "Are you kidding me?!"

Sad to say, there really is not a good way to widen a coach. To cut it down the middle and add spacers in the tunnel, the baggage compartment and the roof bows, in order to move the suspension system outboard, can be structurally disastrous.

The best way to add width is to scab on three inch rectangular tubing to the lower section, then the upper passenger compartment may have the roof bows cut and widened in the center. The principle drawback to this scheme is that now the suspension systems foot print, or stance is still set up for a 96-inch coach carrying a 102-wide coach. The Eagle coach, with its torsion bar suspension and its lateral stability, could probably survive this procedure.

My personal opinion, however, is this is not recommended. If you must have a 102-wide coach, search one out which was engineered by the factory.

Chapter Five

Extendable Floor Space

The latest rage in converting a bus is to create a slide-out room. That is, a section of the body that slides out to add more living space. This will expand your living space by placing the sofa in the slide-out section along with the dinette, and may add up to 45 square feet.

One of the big questions before undertaking such a project is; can it be done structurally without undue reinforcement, and how do you reinforce the structure? Imagine a box beam with a window cut out of one side. This is the situation. Obviously, if you cut a hole out of the side of a box beam (the body of our bus), you need to provide additional structure around the hole to transfer the stresses. These stresses are shear, bending and torsion.

Before we get into a lot of technical talk, I wish to state that Gene Plunk of Medford, Oregon completed a Model 07 Eagle that not only has a 15 foot slide-out, but was also stretched to 45 feet. So, he increased his total living space by nearly one-third. Furthermore, his bus is gorgeous. His living room is like walking into a mansion . . . so spacious and luxurious. Gary Bennett of B & B conversions has successfully completed several slide-out conversions in Las Vegas, NV.

My involvement in this study was as a result of my old buddy, Jack Headley, acquiring a model 10 Eagle with plans to create a slide-out room. Back in the days when I was gainfully employed as an airplane designer, as opposed to being ungainfully employed as a writer, body design was my specialty. So Jack asked me to stress it out, run some numbers, and make some recommendations.

Now, at this point I have to do some editorializing. When solving an engineering problem I can attest, without fear of contradiction, there are a myriad of ways a problem can be solved. If this weren't true there would only be one automobile maker and one airplane manufacture, one washer maker, one toaster maker, etc. One of my axioms is: "There are a gazillion ways to solve an engineering problem, and of these many ways, there might be less than 100,000 solutions equally as good, and probably less than 10,000 that are the best. Therefore, the ideas I am putting forth are only proposals, and I acknowledge there are many ideas that may be better and much more imaginative. How's that for a disclaimer? By the way, Bob Belter, another retired airplane designer, whose articles you may have read in BUS CONVERSIONS magazine, has examined my numbers, and has raised no objections.

The first brush with the numbers was to analyze the truss section running the length of the body from the door line to the window sill. This structure is the primary bending and shear member, supporting the upper body and dumping the load into the lower bulkheads, reacted by the torsion bars and ultimately the axles into the wheels, resting on the ground. Wow, did you follow that? It simply means we have a beam supported at each end. The bending stiffness is not currently dependent on the structure in the baggage section. It is obvious, however, the lateral trusses in the baggage compartment contribute to the torsional stiffness. The bus frame as a whole is what is known as a statically indeterminate structure. We do, however, have ways of determining the indeterminate. What must be done is approximate the size of various structural members, and from that point, determine the stress and strain of the frame. The stresses, of course, are the internal unit

Extendable Floor Space

loading of the materials. The strains are the movement (stretch, or shrinkage), of the frame due to the stresses.

It is important to decide what constitutes a failure condition. Now, if the baggage compartment sags to the ground, this can definitely be considered a failure. If a member buckles or cracks, this too, can be considered a failure. What about some not so obvious failures, like a shear tear-out of a rivet due to a little excessive movement? What about a permanent set in a bending member? Another failure might be excessive movement or misalignment causing the slide-out to bind. I used the criteria of torsional deflection in excess of the original body as a target point. In addition, I attempted to design a stiff frame around the opening that, again, would have no more deflection in bending than the original body.

Although these were noble goals, they were not very practical. The first set of numbers showed that the proposed beam along the bottom of the opening and a plate along the top and ends would fall well under the yield stress of steel, but the deflection due to bending would equal about ten times that of the original frame. And, to solve for that deflection, the bus may have to have several more axles and a lot more fuel capacity just to move. The assumptions listed below were my starting point.

Assumptions:
1. The bus is a model 10 Eagle.
2. Opening size: 60 x 144.
3. Body to be as stiff as original body (this may not be practical).
4. Truss between floor and window sill is the only bending stiffness to be replaced. The header reaction is ignored.
5. The vehicle weight is assumed to be 40,000 lbs.
6. The steering axle weight is assumed to be 12,000

lbs., distributed as 3,000 lbs. per bulkhead per torsion bar, for analysis purposes.

7. The moment reaction of the principal truss is determined by the maximum column load capable by the web compression members.

8. It would be desirable to limit the depth of the reinforcing structure to the depth of the central tunnel, so as to be able to utilize the left hand baggage compartment doors.

9. Frame analysis as suggested by Roark, "Formulas for Stress and Strain", is the criteria.

10. Excessive deflection can be constrained by the use of taper pin latching aligners from the slide-out to the body frame.

After messing around for a few hours with my handy-dandy structural analysis computer programs, I have concluded it would be wise to nest a series of 4" x 4" x 3/8" angles along the left side door section up to the beginning of the wheel well, thus creating an eight by eight inch box beam. This beam will fall well within the elastic limit of hot rolled steel, somewhere around 25,000 psi. From the rear bulkhead of the steering axle wheel well forward, this beam may be reduced to a box beam with a total depth of six inches, thus remaining above the fender opening. This box beam should extend aft to pick up the reaction of at least one bay of the side body truss. On the header section I recommend the use of at least a 4" x 4" x 1/4" angle flanged out nesting on top of the existing header and stitch-welded. This section should be used as the forward vertical frame of the opening. This design will allow a little over one-half inch deflection. This would probably be acceptable when parked since the slide-out section may be designed with tolerance to permit this much movement by the use of seals. And, when the vehicle is in motion, tapered

Extendable Floor Space

latching pins will eliminate deflection and permit the side wall of the slide-out to act as a structural stiffener. This recommended design appears to add about 1,000 pounds to the structural weight of the bus. If a person were willing to accept less height to the left hand side baggage compartment doors, much less deflection would occur and the added weight would be reduced proportionally. As an example, if a 12-inch channel were used in lieu of the box beam, we could probably reduce the weight by forty percent and reduce the deflection to less than 1/2 inch.

As I mentioned above, there are many ways to solve this problem. Perhaps the simplest way would be to create a truss section along the left hand baggage compartment side,

thus eliminating all access to that side except through triangular shaped doors. This approach would surely be the lightest design. So, to use an old buzz word of the sixties, one must make many "trade-off studies" to decide what will suit them. Just remember, any structural problem can be solved, but can you live with the solution? With respect to the Headley bus, we opted to create the lightest solution, which was to create the truss structure in the baggage compartment below the cutout. The picture above illustrates the solution used.

In the picture shown, a pair of rack and pinions were used with a common shaft to maintain uniform extension of the slide-out unit. The unit extended on a set of telescoping slides with ball bearing rollers. The actuator used is a camper screw jack operating on 12VDC and extending 33 inches. The actuation time is 40 seconds, so it is somewhat slow.

Other forms of actuation might be air cylinders, or hydraulic cylinders. These actuators might tend to be a little too fast, and cause an impact situation. Another form of actuator could be a simple sprocket and chain with a 12VDC motor and limit switches. A sprocket and chain set could also be substituted for the rack and pinion to maintain uniform extension.

The slides for this application were a three-tube nested design since Jack did not wish the telescoping supports to extend through the tunnel of the coach. I believe a two tube telescope with nylatron, or polyethylene bearings is a simpler approach.

Chapter Six

Side Hinged Baggage Doors

For those of you who are driving or converting a model-one Eagle, you know the pain[1] and agony of lifting those one-piece baggage doors. And sometimes it is impossible to open them when another vehicle is parked too close or you are forced to park next to a building or fence. Mercifully, Eagle Coach Corporation recognized the problem and re-designed

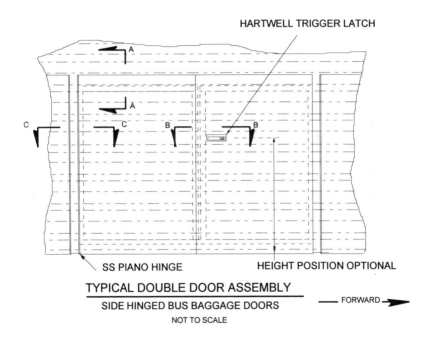

---

[1] Especially when you walk into an open door with your head down.

those baggage doors on their model-five and on, so the doors fold, and in addition have gas cylinder helpers. This is a real breakthrough in design. The newer MCIs and Prevosts not only have the balanced door design, but they lift vertically using a four-bar linkage and lay somewhat flat to the body. You may walk around the coach with reckless abandon, not worrying you might split your head open on a baggage door.

Although the concept described herein, is most applicable to the model-one, it is also very useful for newer Eagle coaches for several reasons. In the first place, to open a side-hinged baggage door requires no more effort than opening a passage door since the weight of the door is supported by the hinge. This feature allows the ladies equal access with minimal effort. The side-hinged door allows total access to the compartment, since the doors may be folded back flat against the bus body. Only one-half of a compartment need be opened in many cases. The coach may be parked as close to a vehicle, building or fence as a human body width and still be able to reach into a compartment. Finally, you may again walk around your coach with your head down and suffer attack only from your mirrors.

The fabrication and construction techniques described in this chapter are only one way of solving the problem. Those of you with access to a sheet metal shop or equipment may wish to fabricate doors by creating a sheet metal pan, and then attaching the extruded siding thereto. For those of you with nothing more complicated than a welder, saw and drill, the process described in this chapter is for you. This is not to say those of you with sophisticated equipment would not benefit by reading further.

Initially, you must determine the size of the steel frame for your doors. If you are working on a model-five or later, all

Side Hinged Baggage Doors

twelve of your door frames will be similar- not alike, only similar. If your coach is a model-one, then you will have eight doors which are similar and four that are similar. The reason for this is you need only one door to cover each of the end openings of the model-one. That is, the 32-inch compartments need only one door each, whereas, the 48-inch compartments are best served with a pair of doors each, hinged on each side like a pair of cabinet doors. On a model-five, or later, all the frames may be identical. The critical dimension to determine is the vertical location of the horizontal bars. The reason for this is you must select an area where the horizontal line of rivets will fall within the flat area of the fluted siding. It would be embarrassing for a horizontal line of rivets to lay on the cusp, or even on the radius of the fluted siding.

TYPICAL SECTION THRU HEADER
SHOWING EXISTING HINGE EXTRUSION

After selecting the height of the frame, determine the width of the frame by allowing a half- inch space between pairs of doors, and the thickness of the hinge folded flat. In the event you are sizing a single door, again, allow one half-inch space to the fixed structure, and the thickness of the hinge. The half-inch is an allowance to install weather sealing. Consideration should be given to whether you wish to keep the existing hinge line extrusion in place or remove it. A more professional job is achieved by removing the old horizontal hinge line extrusion, although it is a job that can try a man's soul. I have done the job both ways at the option of the owner. If you will examine the illustration in Section A-A, option

The Bus Converter's Bible

number 2; it shows the door header with the hinge extrusion removed, showing the door siding faying on an inserted land. To fay means to lay flat or, join tightly.

Once the size of your door frame is determined, they must be fabricated. I use 1 x 1 x .06 square steel tubing. First, I make a welding jig of scrap plywood, or wafer board. This is nothing more than a rectangle of material with another

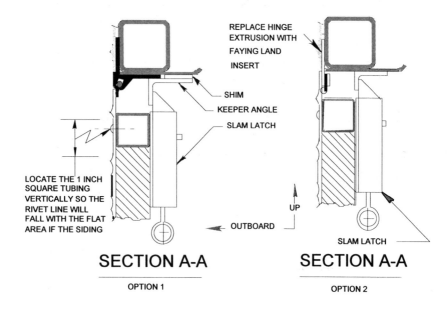

smaller rectangle fastened to the larger piece with a uniform margin all around. The steel tubing is cut to size and clamped to the jig and then welded. A fire or two may break out now and then, but since you are not involved in a high volume production run, the jigs may be discarded after twelve frames are completed. If you have twenty or thirty friends who want side opening doors, you may wish to make steel weld jigs with De-Sta-Co clamps, but I have only done about a half-dozen

Side Hinged Baggage Doors

installations, so I just pitch the ashes when I am done.

Since the doors are very light in weight, the hinges may be aluminum, but I prefer stainless steel piano hinges with an open width of two inches, a pin size of one-eighth inch, and a thickness of at least .040 inches.

The next process is to install the frames. This is when it is important to locate them vertically, so that you have no embarrassing rivet locations, as pointed out earlier. When drilling the hinge for screws, stagger the screw locations from side to side, so that you will not be having screw heads bumping screw heads with the hinge closed. Another approach to installing the frames is to drill holes in the hinges and rosette weld them in place. This approach, however, does not lend itself to any adjustment. We now have our door frames in place, waving in the breeze. We must now install the siding to line up with the existing coach siding.

The next process is to fabricate the siding. This is done by cutting the siding to length with a radial-arm saw. The

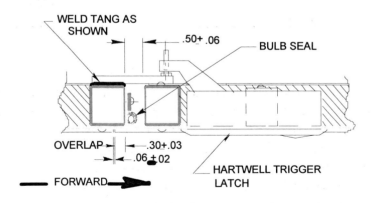

SECTION B-B

material will cut nicely using a carbide toothed saw blade and plenty of cutting oil. The customary cutting oil for aluminum is kerosene. Diesel fuel will work nicely, but I prefer to used WD-40, since it comes in a convenient spray can. If you fail to use some form of cutting oil, the material will gall, clog the saw blade, and create a very ragged cut.

After cutting the material to length, I use a plywood jig to drill and assemble the siding into a door size panel. In the case of a double door, I assemble a single panel to cover both doors. The drill jig is simply a piece of steel bar stock, drilled with pilot holes so the rivets are spaced evenly. Often it is necessary to debur the holes before assembling the pieces of siding. This may be done with a larger drill bit in a handle, or simply turn the panel over and lightly apply a large moving drill bit to each hole. After the double door panel is assembled, it may be run through the table saw with a carbide toothed blade, with plenty of cutting lubricant. You now have a panel for each door. If you will examine the drawing in Section B-B, you will see the leading edge door in a double door set is slightly wider than the trailing edge door. This allows for an approximate 5/16-inch overlap of the leading door onto the trailing door. So the leading door will be slightly over an inch greater in width than the trailing door.

Before clamping the door panels in place and riveting them, determine the location of the door latch, as shown in side view. The door latch I used is a trigger latch made by The Hartwell Corporation of Placentia, California. This is a product of their commercial division and they have distributors across the country. Their Southern California distributor is The R.C. Dudek Co., and their phone number is 1-800-488-1990. The latches are made to fit doors of various thicknesses. The door thickness must be specified, and you may order them all keyed

Side Hinged Baggage Doors

alike. For the past several years, the approximate cost of these latches has been about $ 11.00 each, plus or minus, plus freight, etc. In order for these latches to work, a tang must be secured to the trailing door so the leading door overlaps the tang and the latch then clamps against the tang.

The trailing door is normally secured with a slam latch shown in Section A-A. Slam latches are quite common and may be obtained where truck body parts are sold. They have a spring loaded, tapered striker which will retract when slammed, and extend on the other side of a keeper plate, or angle. They are generally about six to seven dollars each.

After the siding is riveted in place, a rigid foam is installed inside the frame for noise control. Of course, the foam will also serve as a thermal insulation. Finally, an inside skin is applied with rivets and the installation is nearly complete. It

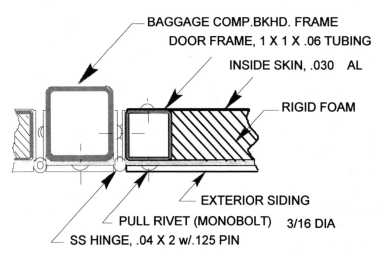

SECTION C-C

is a good idea to add seals to keep the weather out. These seals are available from home improvement stores, and come in many shapes and sizes. The selection is not critical since almost any form of weather stripping will work.

If you have fabricated your door frames from square tubing, you will probably have a set of tubes open from one end to the other. I simply glued small squares of aluminum skin to the open tubes with silicone. If you used steel skin for the inside of the doors, you may want to prime and paint them, but if you used aluminum they may be left as is, your choice.

Chapter Seven

The Steel Case

    Back in my earlier days, while making a living as one of several hundred lowly designers hunched over a drawing board in a design room of a major fabricator of airframe structures, I remember the beginning of a poem that commonly circulated. It began like this:

> *I made a wooden airplane,*
> *but it wooden fly*
> *I made a steel airplane,*
> *but it steel wooden fly*
> *................*

Although, this introduction has nothing to do with the subject of this dissertation, I include it because it contains the chapter subject, steel.

    After many modifications to our bus structures, such as, raising the roof, stretching the coach, adding slide-outs , and so on, it becomes necessary to provide a new integument skin, siding, or whatever you wish to call it. A strong argument, and a natural inclination is to use aluminum. Why? Well, the argument is it is lighter, easier to fabricate, and much of the original shell was covered in aluminum, and it looks good. Another popular material under consideration is fiberglass. Again, because fiberglass is light, easy to fabricate, and takes paint and Bondo well. Stand by, as I intend to scuttle most of these alleged facts and make the case for common cold rolled mild steel.

    In the first place, aluminum is not lighter than steel from a stiffness stand point. And, if you want a smooth skin without all kinds of "oil cans" (another term for buckles and wrinkles), you must consider the stiffness of the siding between the structural members, or stiffeners. It may surprise many of my readers to learn aluminum and steel have the same stiffness. Stiffness is defined as the product of the Modulus of Elasticity times the thickness of the material. Now, I realize this all sounds like a lot of gobbledegook, so let me simplify. The Modulus of Elasticity is the amount of stretch a material will experience for a unit load. Consider this: if you load the same size of steel bar and aluminum bar with the same amount of tensile load, you will see that the aluminum will stretch three times that of the steel.

Just so we will have some real numbers to talk about, the E_S, (Modulus of Elasticity) for steel is about 30 million pounds per square inch[1], (psi). Aluminum E_A= 10,000,000 psi. So now we understand Aluminum E_A is about one-third of Steel E_S. Another interesting fact is the weight of aluminum is about one-third that of steel. The weight of aluminum is one-tenth of a pound per cubic inch, and the weight of steel is three-tenths of a pound per cubic inch. So, the obvious statement is that steel is three times heavier than aluminum, right? In the same thickness, this is true.

So now, lets pick a material thickness for our new siding. If we select 18 gage steel, (.040 inch), how thick must we chose if we want to use aluminum? To achieve equal stiffness with aluminum, we must choose 12 gage,(.120 inch). Why? The stiffness is **E x t,** so for steel **S** (stiffness) = 30,000,000 x .040 = 1,200,000 pound per inch. The gage for aluminum, $t_a = E_s t_s/E_a$ = .120 inch.

---

[1] The reason the word "about" is used, is there is a slight variation in the modulus of elasticity between various alloys.

The Steel Case

Now here is where it gets interesting. The weight of steel is **0.3** pci (pounds per cubic inch), and that of aluminum is **0.1** pci. So steel will weigh .3 x .040 x 144 = **1.72** pounds per square foot, and aluminum will weigh .1 x .12 x 144 = **1.72** pounds per square foot. So now we have proved that aluminum and steel to have equal stiffness must weigh the same.

OK, we will now examine other criteria besides stiffness. How about investigating thermal expansion. Each material has another property known as the **coefficient of thermal expansion,** (ϵ). Simply put, each rigid material will grow or shrink according to the temperature in which it dwells. The simplest definition of the coefficient of thermal expansion is the rate of change in inches per inch per degree Fahrenheit. Another way to put it is an inch of material will grow a specific amount for each increase of one degree of temperature.

For the record, the ϵ_s, (coefficient of expansion of steel) = 0.0000063, and the ϵ_a = 0.0000125. This sure looks like a lot of zeros behind the decimal point, so does it really make any difference? Lets assume that a bus is 40 feet, or 480 inches, and we apply our skin at about 70 degrees. One day, we decide to go camping at Furnace Creek in Death Valley. We arrive with a nice comfortable temperature of 85, but the next day the temperature goes up to 120 degrees. Under these conditions, our bus framework will grow 0.0000063 x 480 x 50^2= 0.152 inch. This is only about 5/32th of an inch, a little over an 1/8th of an inch, so what's the big deal? Lets see how much our aluminum side has grown. Aluminum expansion = 0.0000125

---

[2]The temperature difference between the application temperature and the outside temperature at Death Valley

x 480 x 50 = 0.300 inch. This really isn't much of a difference, or is it? The actual difference will be 0.148 inch, or a little over an 1/8th of an inch difference. Where is the extra aluminum going to go? It can't extend beyond the coach, so it has no choice but to buckle, or create *oil cans*. Now this problem can be solved in two ways.

The first solution is to install the aluminum in a pre-stressed condition, as described in an earlier article in BUS CONVERSION magazine by Bob Belter, *The Bus Skinner*. The only drawback to this is the material must be heated so that it will expand and then be riveted while it is still hot. In addition, over time the material will creep, and due to cycling, will eventually relax. Then we are back to the wrinkles and buckling. Furthermore, this pre-stress must be reacted by the rivets in shear. And, after many cycles the rivets tend to loosen. So, you may ask, how does Eagle Coach Corporation get by using aluminum for it's lower siding? If you will examine the lower siding you will notice it is fluted, or convoluted with cusps adding to the panel as little stiffeners. These little stiffeners are about 3/16th of an inch in thickness, so all they have to stiffen is the span between the framework, or a maximum distance of about 27 inches. So the strain (or growth of aluminum siding), caused by 50 degrees of temperature rise over 27 inches is only about 0.0168 inches, but the growth of the steel frame over this distance would be .0085 inches, or a difference of 0.008 inches. This would cause a compression stress in the aluminum, therefore causing the siding to act as a flat column. From this difference in strain (or growth) we may calculate the stress, and hence the column loading due to the temperature rise. The small stiffeners added to the siding are adequate to resist this deformation, or buckling. If you will notice the fluting along the

The Steel Case

side of the venerable old GM 4104 or 4106, you will see ribbing in a longitudinal manner. This too allows the siding to remain relatively flat. Therefore, the second solution is to increase the thickness, or provide ribbing or small stiffeners to prevent *oil cans*. The MCIs and Prevosts have always used steel, stainless steel that is, of quite thin gauge with formed stiffeners.

Now, let us examine fiberglass as a siding material. The E_f value (modulus of elasticity) for fiberglass and most structural plastics is about 1,200,000 psi. This is around one-eighth of aluminum and about one-twenty-fourth of steel. So, what does this mean? Simply put, it means fiberglass acts like a rubbery material compared to the metals, since it is eight times more elastic than aluminum and more than twenty-four times more elastic than steel. For example, to make fiberglass equal in stiffness to 0.040 steel, it will have to be at least one -inch thick. However, experience has shown fiberglass backed up with 1/2 inch plywood will maintain a smooth flat side. This of course will cause the siding to be outside of original contour of the coach by one-half inch. If you simply try to stiffen fiberglass by applying it to the framework, and then bond plywood to the inside of the framework, each steel frame will print through and the appearance of your coach will certainly be out of the ordinary. Many of the motorhome manufacturers use fiberglass, but do so bonded over plywood, with the complete assembly attached over the framework.

This now brings me to the simplest solution of all. Use steel for your flat skin between windows, or wherever you wish. Remember, 18 gauge steel has the same stiffness as 12 gauge aluminum. It will weigh the same and it will cost approximately one-third of aluminum. That is, a pound of steel will cost about 65 cents, compared to about $ 2.25 for aluminum. Steel finishes nicely. Detroit and Japan have been using it for years on luxury cars, and cheap cars (?) too. The major argument for using steel, besides cost, is it will grow at the same rate as the frame of the bus as the temperature changes, hence there is no worry of buckled siding.

Steel also has the advantage of offering several ways of attaching the material to the bus. The obvious way is to use rivets. Steel or aluminum are acceptable. What about electrolysis? Add a small amount of sealant between the skin and the frame. Since electrolysis needs an electrolyte to function, and by keeping the inside of the materials dry, you probably won't experience a significant level of electrolysis for about 700 years. You may then have to replace the siding.

The next possible way if you wish to have smooth siding with no rivets showing, is to weld the steel to the bus frame. If you have access to the wire feed welder (and all bus converters should have), simply drill 1/4 inch holes about every four inches over the bus frame in the siding, snug the siding against the frame and fill the hole with weld metal. This is also known as rosette welding. Or if you have access to a spot welder, use it. The principle advantage of the wire feed, or the spot welder, is a minimum heat can be used which will minimize distortion. Regardless, a little bit of body work will be required around the welds, since it is impossible to avoid a little distortion. An example of this technique is the bus converted by Ed Taylor of Bakersfield, CA. It is a beautifully done Eagle with absolutely smooth steel siding.

Finally, if you are a sporting kind, you may bond your new siding in place with a Urethane adhesive bonding material. SikaFlex 252 is recommended for adhesive bonding of bus panels, and is probably at least twice the strength of aluminum rivets. In addition, adhesive bonding maintains a smooth uniform stress condition, as opposed to a series of multiple stress concentration points caused by riveting. Adhesive bonding, which has for years been used in aircraft fabrication, will be the subject of a future revision to this book.

The Bus Converter's Bible

Notes:

Sketches

Chapter Eight

Swing-out Radiator for the Eagle Coach

A little over thirty years ago, *Maintainability* was the buzz word in the aircraft design rooms. As an example, the wings and the engine nacelle could almost be disassembled for access, and although it cost weight (a precious commodity in aircraft performance), access panels were created where needed to enhance and facilitate maintenance.

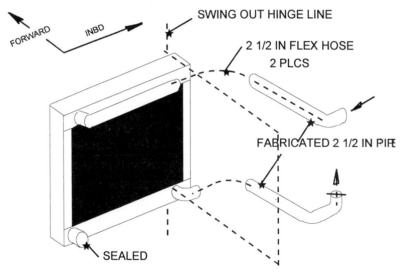

SILVER EAGLE SWING-OUT RADIATOR CONCEPT
by D. W. GALEY 8-3-94

The modern Eagle coach has made an effort toward this goal with its swing-out A/C condenser, floor hatches, and engine access doors. However, with its engine offset by seven inches and its permanently mounted radiator, access to the street side of the motor is not easy. We have tried to remedy this by the development of a swing-out radiator.

My personal coach is a Model 05 Eagle, which was converted to a motorhome about seven years ago. I previously had a converted Model-01 Eagle, which was used for about eight years. With both these conversions, the down-the-road air conditioning was removed and a Ten-KW generator installed in its location, mounted in a swing-out support to provide access to the bus engine. In addition, a rear floor section over the motor was cut out to create a four by five foot engine hatch under the bed, an option not available for a passenger coach. After driving nearly 200,000 miles in the U.S., Mexico and Canada, from time to time breakdowns have occurred and I have been thankful for the easy access to the motor. Once, while going through Chicago, I noticed a slight drop in oil pressure, so I pulled over to the shoulder and checked the oil. The dip stick showed about a gallon over, so I found a Detroit-Allison shop, and in short order they located and replaced a broken fuel line inside the curbside valve cover. Again I was thankful for the swing-out generator. If the failure had been on the other side, I would have had to raise the bed and stretch protective paper down the length of the bus to protect the floor covering. The process would have cost additional time, inconvenience, and service charges. So the idea of the swing-out radiator began to take shape. The following is a description of our solution.

Initially the coolant was drained from the system and the hoses were removed. The coolant was drained into a fifteen-gallon tub since its reuse was planned, because it contained not only antifreeze but was conditioned with Nalcool 3000.

If you measure the diagonal dimension of the radiator in plan view, it appears it will not clear the available opening. However, a judicious selection of the hinge line allowed the idea to work. Hinges were fabricated using quarter inch bar stock and

Swing-Out Radiator

three-quarter inch mechanical tubing with eighth inch wall thickness using a six-inch by half-inch grade five bolt for the hinge pin. A hinge post was installed using a two by two by quarter inch angle welded to the frame work forward of the radiator. With the radiator in its original position, two hinges were welded to the radiator frame and to the hinge post. The lower bus frame, to which the radiator pan is attached, was then sawn at each end of the radiator door opening. This now allowed the pan to drop permitting the radiator to swing out. Obviously it cannot swing out, since it is still attached to the bus mounting points. The eight bolts on each side of the radiator were removed. A cutting torch was used to remove the quarter inch plate at the rear of the radiator. This was done carefully to preserve the surrounding structure. At this point, the only thing preventing the radiator assembly from swinging out is the fan shroud, or bellmouth as it is sometimes called. This became the biggest glitch in the approach. If it were done again, the radiator should first be removed, then the bellmouth, the radiator re-installed and the procedure outlined above followed. A swing-out condition was achieved, however, by a little persuasive body work on the shroud, but it is better to avoid this step. The next procedure was to fabricate a rear support system, since the quarter inch supporting plate was removed. This was done by cutting down the existing support plate to a four-bolt pattern size and hinging it so it would attach to the radiator frame as before, but swing away to allow the assembly to swing out. The forward support plate was left in place and the upper four bolts were used for the forward radiator support. Since the scheme is to permit the radiator to swing out without draining the coolant and the total weight of radiator and coolant are supported only on one end, a diagonal tension rod was added to the radiator frame to avoid distortion, thus preventing a leak. We now have a hinged radiator assembly.

The next project was to create a plumbing system which will allow the radiator to function, but is hingeable without the need for expensive swivel joints. Ideally, the plumbing should be either copper or aluminum tubing, but in this case galvanized steel tubing (chainlink fence post) was used. Since the radiator was hinged at the forward end the coolant was routed forward from both the engine port and the radiator so a flexible radiator hose could be used. The upper lines, or hot water lines, were fairly easy and straight forward; simply ninety degree bends approximately two feet in length to which the flexible hose was attached. A joggle in the upper section radiator side was necessary to avoid a fitting on the radiator. The lower section of the radiator contains two return ports. The rearmost port was simply sealed and a short ninety degree section was used on the forwardmost port. The fixed return pipe to the engine water pump had several joggles in order to avoid both the fan and the bus structure and still line up with the engine water pump. All of the rigid plumbing lay between the bus frame structure and the frame side of the bellmouth. The hoses were then installed and the coolant replaced. Tabs were welded to the bottom of the frame attaching the pan assembly and nuts were welded inside of the fixed structure so the pan frame could be bolted in place. This now required ten bolts be removed before the radiator assembly could be swung out for engine access. With a half-inch air impact wrench, the operation takes about ten minutes.

The installation was then test driven, and we were somewhat surprised to see the temperature gauges were reading a little on the low side. As of this writing, we have a little over 10,000 miles on the installation in both desert and mountainous driving, and have concluded under moat conditions the bus is running somewhere between five and ten degrees cooler. I must say

Swing-Out Radiator

as we went by Las Vegas whose outside temperature was 115 degrees, it performed as it normally would, hot. This cooler running is probably attributable to the longer piping and attendant bends causing a pressure drop and allowing the coolant to dwell longer in the core, thus giving up more Btus in the process. As a matter of interest, it is suggested that almost any competent shop could accomplish this modification for about 24 labor hours and about one hundred dollars in parts. The use of copper plumbing may increase the cost a little but not significantly.

The Bus Converter's Bible

Notes:

Sketches

Chapter Nine

HINGED UTILITY SUPPORT STRUCTURE

Often we would like to mount a device on a support system which would swing out for accessibility. More specific applications would be a tool box mounted in our baggage compartment, or a generator mounted in such a way we would have access for servicing, or the ability to service something being blocked by the unit. The sliding approach would solve the problem, but would still tend to block access behind the

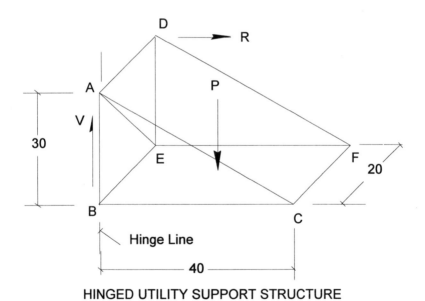

HINGED UTILITY SUPPORT STRUCTURE

unit. So, a single hinge line, allowing the entire support to rotate would be more facilitating.

The illustration shown is a typical design with the hinge

line located along the line **A - B**. The dimensions shown are in inches and are chosen as a typical application for a generator support structure in a baggage compartment, or the right rear compartment of an Eagle.

For simplicity, we might select a design composed of 1½ inch x 3/16 inch steel angles, welded in the shape shown. Let us further assume that we wish to support a powerplant weighing 400 pounds. We would soon discover that the principle design flaw would be the sagging, or deflection at point **F** as a result of gravity. And, if point **F** sags, then it follows that point **D** will rotate in a clockwise direction. As undesirable as these results are, they are easily corrected by the use of a torsion member located along the hinge line.

The solution to the torsion stresses are somewhat complex, and a little bit boring, but is presented here for those of you wishing to verify the beauty of simple design. Those of you not wishing to follow the mathematics may skip to the end of this discussion, and be confident of using your gut instincts, or cut and try to satisfy the design problem.

The vertical hinge loads are represented by the letter **V**, and are equal to the vertical load **P**. In addition, the hinge line also feels a rotating moment distributed in a triangular fashion with the upper half in tension and the lower half in compression. The torsion loads are computed by solving for the horizontal reaction **R** at point **D**. With the geometry shown **R= ⅓P**. The computed deflection of the arm **A - D** will be $Pl^3/9EI$, where P is the load, l is the length of the arm **A - D**, E is the modulus of elasticity, and I is the section moment of inertia. In our example the horizontal deflection, or rotation of point **D** is **0.098** inches, or less than a tenth of an inch. This appears to be satisfactory. Now let us examine the torsional deflection, or the rotation of point **D** due to the torsional resistance (or lack thereof) of the vertical member along the hinge line.

The equation to determine the rotation of a bar is expressed in radians and is:

Theta (Radians) =**Tl/KG**, where **T** = Torsional moment, or twisting load

l = the length of the member (in our case, the length of the hinge line, 30 inches)

K = a factor determined by the shape of the member

G = the modulus of rigidity (for steel= 11.5×10^6)

The **K** factor for our 1½ inch steel angle is = 0.00855^1

So the equation for the angular twist results in a number of **0.785** radians, or nearly **45 degrees!** Obviously, this is totally unacceptable. So lets investigate the use of a pipe or a piece of tubing along the hinge line, and re-calculate the angular twist.

The **K** factor for a solid round bar is =**Pir^4/2**, for a hollow round bar or a pipe, the equation is **K = Pi/2(r_1^4 - r_2^4)**. For a tube 1½ inch in diameter, and a wall thickness of 1/16 inch, the **K** factor = 3.21. Using this factor in the equation for twisting, we find that the point **D** will move **0.00216** radians, or about one-eighth of a degree. This translates into a total movement of about **1/16** of an inch. This is totally acceptable.

The equation for K of an angle is as follows:

$K=K_1+K_2+t^4$, where $K_1=bt^3\{⅓- .21t/b[1-t^4/12b^4]\}$

$K_2=bt^3\{⅓- .105t/b[1-t^4/192b^4]\}$

b = length of angle leg, and t= thickness

This illustration also shows that the steel angle weighing five pounds is incapable of performing in this application, whereas a simple tube weighing only two and a half pounds is satisfactory.

Returning to our design, it may be more practical to use a slightly thicker walled tube than the one in the example above. A standard black iron pipe, 1 ¼ IPS, would be more appropriate and easier to weld. Along more mundane considerations, the HUSS (hinged utility support structure) should be designed to ride up on a ramp in order to eliminate

all traveling loads.

The photograph above shows a semi-symmetrical support for a generator hanging on a one inch steel rod supported by pillow blocks (Courtesy, Marvin Zepede).

Ref: Formulas for Stress and Strain, Raymond J. Roark, 4th ed.

Part Two

Plumbing

The Bus Converters' Bible

Chapter Ten

Introduction to Plumbing

This section on fresh water plumbing systems for bus conversions to motor homes is presented to acquaint a prospective owner of the various options available when planning a bus conversion. Although the options in a water supply system are as varied as those in a residential installation, and limited only by space and imagination, a common and universal concept is displayed. We have included a typical universal schematic for a bus conversion fresh water system.

Most states have code requirements pertaining to plumbing installations so it would be advisable to check with your local state Department of Housing to obtain this code, assuming you are not already familiar with the codes. Additionally, the Recreational Vehicle Industry Association (RVIA) has established standards that satisfy the various jurisdictional requirements. Refer to the message in the introduction page 14, for addresses and publication number.

We will explore the various materials commonly available for the components, fittings recommended and fixtures available. Since each chapter will discuss the components referred to in the illustration on the following page, the schematic shown will be repeated at a smaller scale.

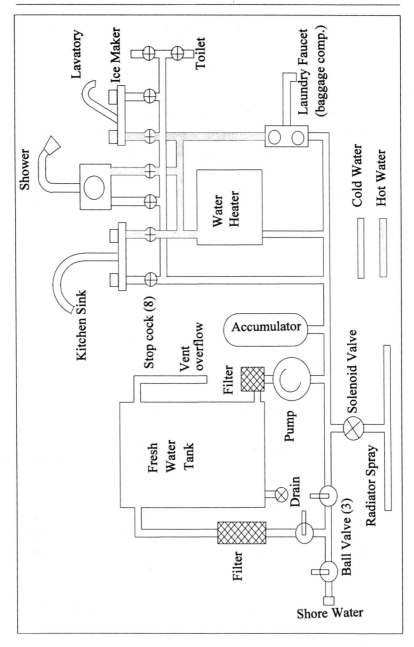

Chapter Eleven

Materials

Plumbing in a Bus/Motorhome conversion is not much different than the plumbing we have in our homes. The principle difference is we carry our water supply and our waste water with us until we replenish our water and dump our waste. The material we use does cover a broad spectrum, however.

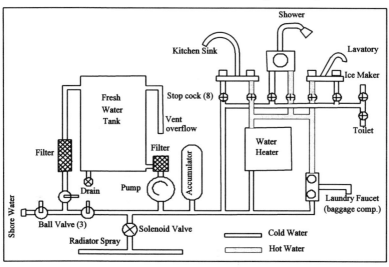

Drain, or waste piping, is generally ABS (acronitrile-butadene-styrene), or PVC (polyvinylchloride). On the other hand, our options are quite varied when it comes to fresh water supply. Copper with sweat fittings, also known as soldered joints, is quite desirable, but must be well insulated in the unheated areas such as the baggage compartments. And even in sub zero weather, freeze-ups can occur. Ordinary PVC or plastic pipe is acceptable, and easy to install, but may not be used for hot water applications. Moreover, plastic pipe can withstand colder temperatures than copper without bursting due to freezing. Another form of plastic pipe is CPVC (Copolyvinylchloride) and is specifically designed to operate under all residential environments including hot water applications and performs similar to PVC in cold weather. Of course, there is iron and galvanized pipe, but it is not recommended due to its weight and troublesome installation. A relatively new product (within the last 20 years) is QUEST pipe, which is a form of CPVC plastic. This material was developed for the mobile home industry and is able to withstand all normal temperatures. What's more, all the fittings in QUEST are compression style and may be installed hand tight. So the tools required are minimal, simply a pipe cutter. Another option is the black nylon DOT, (U.S.Department of Transportation) air brake line. This material is available in sizes up to 3/4 inch diameter and is able to withstand all normal temperatures. It uses simple sleeves, ferrules, and compression fittings. Finally, there is an incident of copper piping in a baggage compartment which froze and burst in sub-zero weather and was replaced in an emergency with a heater hose and hose clamps. Later the heater hose was simply replaced with food grade hose slipped over the stub ends of the half-inch copper pipe and clamped. It has been serving quite satisfactorily since.

    Which ever material is chosen, consider the environment, ease of installation, and ease of maintenance. Plumbing piping in a standard residence is chosen and installed to last indefinitely. The goal in a motorhome conversion should be the same. Keep in mind that a motorhome will experience all sorts of weather. It is subject to vibration, and possible movement of the piping. When hooking up to shore water, pressure may vary from 40 pounds to 180 pounds. Remember that an elbow or a tee in a high pressure situation is trying to separate proportional to the water pressure. For example, if the water pressure is 200 psi on a half-inch compression tee, the separation force is 40 pounds. Many plastic fittings cannot withstand that much of a pull. If the pipe is one inch, the separation force is nearly 160 pounds. A sensible procedure is to install a pressure regulator at the shore water hook-up point that will limit the coach water pressure to 50 psi, or less. The standard water pumps for motorhomes are set to provide 35 psi water pressure. This amount of pressure is adequate for all normal applications.

It may be useful to mix materials in the installation. If, for example there are areas which will ultimately be inaccessible be it a benign environment, a more permanent material such as copper, or even stainless steel or galvanized pipe might be appropriate. This may be in areas behind cabinets or other pipe chases which tend to become permanently enclosed. In choosing materials keep in mind not only ease of installation, but maintainability. You or your converter may hope to never see the plumbing again once it is installed, but anything mechanical can break down. If this happens miles from the installer, you or your builder should design the installation so that it can be repaired by a mechanic unfamiliar with the system. This is a case for a complete schematic drawing to be kept with the important papers of your coach. Finally, economics must be considered. The finest installation using the most expensive AeroQuip steel reinforced hose is certainly going to function for years, but is quite expensive and definitely an overkill.

To summarize, the material available for plumbing are:

```
ABS      ...... drain, vent and waste.
PVC      ...... drain, vent, waste, and water
CPVC     ...... fresh water
QUEST ....................... fresh water
Copper, sweat fittings    ...... fresh water
Copper, comp. fittings    ...... fresh water
Black iron pipe ................. gas, LPG
Galvanized iron pipe ............ fresh water
Food grade hose ................ water
Black DOT nylon tubing ......... water
```

There are many other optional materials, but practicality must be considered. For example, you wouldn't want to use a high pressure hydraulic hose for an application this simple, or AeroQuip steel braid reinforced tubing. Although there is a coach using the nylon DOT air line for its water system. Even this application is a little questionable. There is no one absolute material to be used for plumbing. Consider your service, environment, installation, maintainability, and economics.

Chapter Twelve

Fresh Water Tankage

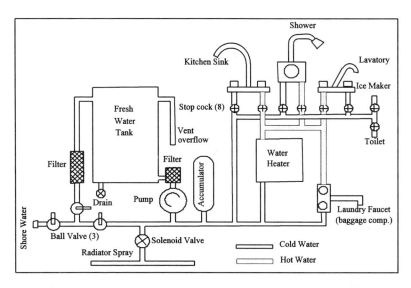

    The Figure above shows a typical fresh water system for bus conversion. Modifications to this scheme are in order for any atypical application. For example, it is a good idea to provide a back-up water pump in the event of a failure of the primary pump. This is simply done by adding another pump in parallel with the primary pump and adding an extra switch. This *back-up* pump as shown on page 86 may also be considered a dual pump system. In our personal coach we have had this feature in place for over five years. Although it was designed originally as a back-up pump, it was also felt it may be used to increase the water flow by turning both on simultaneously. This idea was planned to provide more luxurious showers. We have one 3.1 gpm, (gallons per minutes) pump, and one 2.8 gpm pump. Each pump singularly seems to produce about 2.5 gpm. With both pumps on, we achieve a little over 4.0 gallons per minute. For *boondocking,* or dry-camping, we don't recommend this extravagant use of water.

Additional fixtures may be added by picking up a hot and cold water line from any convenient place and routing to the additional fixture. Where the diagram shows a solenoid to control the water spray to the radiator, another pump may be substituted just down stream of the tank exit filter. Just route the switch to the cockpit for the driver's control. Moreover, if another radiator is used, just tee-off downstream of the solenoid to the other radiator. Why have a water spray on your radiator? It is comforting while on long grades to cool your engine by spraying water on your radiator.

The water storage tank is the largest piece of equipment. Here the owner must decide both the material and the size. Recently, polyethelene and polypropylene have become the most popular choice of tank materials. The fabrication process is rotational molding, which is a process of loading the mold with beads of the material, heating the mold and rotating so that as the material melts and it is centrifugally deposited to the outer surface of the mold. This has the advantage of creating substantial fillets in the corners of a rectangular box where the strength is needed. The fittings are spin welded in place at any location the customer wishes. An injection molded fitting is attached to a fixture on a hand router, spun on a pre-drilled location, then the friction heat causes the fitting and the tank wall to fuse in place. The disadvantage to this material for tanks is that you must accept the size of tanks for which molds are available. You might have a mold fabricated for you, but unless you plan to go into production of coaches with similar layouts, this is not cost effective.

Fresh Water Tankage

Catalogs are available from suppliers listing a variety of sizes. Most of these tanks do not exceed 100 gallon capacity.

Other tank materials available are fiberglass, and plywood coated fiberglass. This has the advantage of being able to custom fabricate tanks to accommodate any shape or space. The greatest drawback is the potential for leakage in the plastic and subsequent rot and odor for the wood material. The polyester resin to use in tank application is known a isothalic, as opposed to orthothalic, in that isothalic polyester has greater corrosion resistance. These materials are highly technical and require a large measure of talent to fabricate, so it is recommended a professional be used. Contrary to popular belief, it is definitely not a do-it-yourself material.

Common black iron may be used to weld fabricate tanks. Although black iron is prone to corrosion, a sloshing technique has been used to coat the interior with food grade plastic to make the tanks last for fresh water applications. The labor to weld fabricate black iron is no different than it would be to make a stainless steel tank, and this would require no sloshing process. So, even though it is more expensive than black iron, the top of the line in tankage material would be type 302 stainless steel. Although there are numerous grades of stainless steel, 300 series, 400 series and PH series, the most common grade for corrosion resistance is 302. This material is also known as 18-8 steel containing 18 percent chromium, and 8 percent nickel. 302-SS is easily fabricated using the same techniques to fabricate carbon steels. The final cost would probably not exceed the cost of an iron tank by twenty-five percent.

If a plastic tank is desired that is much larger than 100 gallons, polypropylene may be purchased in 4' by 8' sheets in thicknesses of 3/8-inch, 1/2-inch, and up. These materials are then welded using special heat guns, and the corners are filleted to reinforce them. These tanks, because of the high cost of the material, can be very expensive but do have the added advantage of being translucent so as to be able to see the liquid level. This allows the user to know exactly their water status without the need for monitoring equipment.

The size of the water storage tank must be determined by the user and the way they plan to use their conversion. If the coach use will primarily be in campgrounds and parks where water is readily available, the tank may be quite small. Since even though the plans are to park in campgrounds, an occasional overnight occurs on the road, such as a rest stop or shopping center parking lot, so it is recommended to have at least 80 gallons of fresh water capacity. Also, if you plan to use your water supply to cool your radiator, be sure your tanks are topped off. In Southern California most of the charter bus companies install a 55 gallon drum with its own pump to provide radiator cooling as they make the run to and from Las Vegas. One desert stretch known as the Baker grade on I-15 is a 17 mile up hill pull at from five to six percent, from sea level to over 4000 ft. This is a real bus killer. Radiator water spray in the summer time is mandatory. If you plan to do a lot of dry-camping, that is, outside of campgrounds and away from facilities, install the largest tank you can squeeze in. Two hundred gallons will allow two people to shower every other day, use the toilets, and in general be water wasters for about two weeks. This does not permit much allowance for the radiator. To ballpark various usages is really hard to do, since it varies with each ones lifestyle. A shower can take from 5 to 10 gallons. The toilet is no more than a gallon per flush. To wash dishes may use 1 to 2 gallons. Cooking and drinking takes about a gallon per day per person. So the best rule is to estimate for bathing, cooking, drinking, engine cooling, and simply put in all you can.

Consideration should be given to the location of both the

Fresh Water Tankage

fresh water tank and the waste tank(s). Keep in mind water weighing 62.4 pounds per cubic foot, or 8.35 pounds per gallon, that a 150 gallon tank full of water has a weight of over 1250 pounds. If we were mechanical people, what would be removed from the fresh water tank would be deposited into the waste water tank. Although, this is not the case, there is some argument because we take in extra drinks in the form of cokes, beer and other drinks, we need more in waste holding than in fresh water capacity. On the other hand, often we take advantage of public facilities, so the argument may go either way. In any event, since the weight of the tankage is a significant factor in the overall weight of the coach, it is recommended the tankage, regardless of the size, be located as near to the center of gravity of the coach as is practical. The center of gravity of the Eagle coach is approximately 17 inches forward of the rear baggage bulkhead. All motor coaches have the passenger capacity of approximately 50 people with their baggage. This yields an approximate pay load of 9,000 pounds. And since, the driver allows the passengers to sit anywhere they choose, with a light load, say ten people, the coach continues to be stable and manageable. Regardless of the preceding argument, it is best if the tankage were clustered close to the center of gravity.

    One other consideration when installing your tanks, is to insulate them. This is especially useful for your fresh water when traveling through a very hot area which may heat the water in the tanks. It is very pleasant to have cool water for drinking. It may also save a tank low on water from freezing.

The Bus Converter's Bible

Notes:

Sketches

Chapter Thirteen

Fittings and Equipment

In this section on fittings and equipment, we will refer to such items as valves, pumps, stop cocks and filters. The discussion will lead from the shore water hook-up point through to the various plumbing fixtures, such as the faucets and water appliances as shown in the diagram.

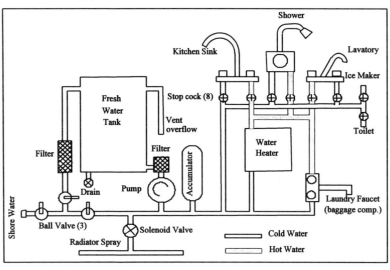

At the shore water hook-up point we use a standard female hose connection which may be adapted to the form of piping used. The standard location of the shore water attach point is near the center of gravity of the coach on the left side. This is the location of all camp ground hook-up utilities, such as water, sewer, electrical, TV cable and telephone. Other options at this point, are quick disconnect fittings made either of plasticorbrass. The advantage of using this form of fitting is the female end is left on the coupling hose, and when it is attached to the vehicle with its built-in "O" ring sealing system, it seldom leaks. Often, using a plain hose connection, pliers must be used to insure against leakage. Just downstream of the shore connection, it is advisable to install a pressure regulator to compensate for potentially disastrous water pressures. We need only about 30 to 50 psi for normal usage.

The drawing shows three ball valves just downstream from the shore water connection. The object is to facilitate filling the tank and, of course providing potable water while in a camp ground. Traditionally, a check valve is used just behind the entry point instead of the first ball valve. Check valves have a tendency to fail, or leak slightly. They are not to be trusted. This is especially true of the inexpensive products sold in the RV market. Any kind of positive sealing valve would work in this location. A gate valve is not recommended because of size and its tendency to seep. The advantage to the ball valve is unobstructed flow, positive sealing, and compact size.

The diagram shows three ball valves. So while coupled to the shore tap, the valve leading to the tank is closed and the first and third valves are open, thereby providing pressure to the system. The water delivery pump is activated with a low pressure switch so with line pressure it remains dormant. To fill the tank while attached to the shore water the valve leading to the tank is opened, and the third valve is closed. The reason for closing the third valve is with no pressure in the system the pump will activate and simply recirculate water from the tank to the tank while it is being filled. Finally, valve number one should be closed before the shore water is disconnected in order to return to a self-contained system.

The optional filter up stream of the water tank is to filter gross material from entering the storage tank. The small filter ahead of the pump is to trap any sand or particulate which might foul the pump. This small sand filter is mandatory to maintain pump life and preventing the pump from failing altogether. Other filters may be installed further down the system on the cold water line just prior to the ice maker or the kitchen faucet for drinking water. Many filters are available and most are quite remarkable in their performance. Much of the advance in water filter design is a result of research directed toward our space program. The cost of the reverse osmosis system of water purification has dropped remarkably in recent years, however, to be effective, this system must be connected to a source of water pressure of at least 50 pounds per square inch. Since our normal RV water pumps deliver only about 35 psi, we must eliminate the reverse osmosis purification system from our consideration. Although every effort is made to avoid recommending specific products by trade name, a space age water filter which is a small stainless steel canister, and marketed under the name **Sea Gull**, is not only acceptable for those on low sodium diets, but exceptionally effective in filtering out the smallest bacteria.

The accumulator is nothing more than a hydraulic spring to absorb the pulsations of the water pump. A standard unit available from RV supply companies is a pre-charged water tank with a bladder, so air pressure over the water may be inflated to a compensating pressure. It comes pre-charged to about 15 psi (pounds per square inch) and is approximately 10 inches in diameter and 10 inches long. The action taking place is: water fills the tank to a certain level until the trapped air, or bladder, prevents more water from entering, which balances the output pressure of the pump. This compressed air, or the expanded bladder, acts as a spring and absorbs the pulsation of the pump. Furthermore, water is often delivered to the faucet without the pump operating.

Another pump may be substituted for the solenoid valve shown on the diagram to supply cooling water to the radiator spray. No accumulator is necessary in this application since pulsing water would have no effect on the radiator. However, if the solenoid were left as shown, the single accumulator would accommodate the entire system.

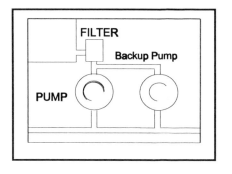

The vent/overflow piping should penetrate to the outside, preferably through the bottom of the vehicle. Depending on the size of the tank, filling a large tank with water can exceed a half hour, and it is easy to become distracted during this time, so the vent not only serves to exhaust air from the tank and permit water to supply the pump, it can also serve as an overflow in case another more interesting project arises. Rarely is it necessary to drain the water tank, but a simple fitting with a pipe cap is all that is required. If one wishes, a drain cock may be used for this application.

Stop cocks, or angle cocks as they are also known, should be used just up stream of each fixture, ie., each faucet,

Fittings and Equipment

mixing valve, or appliance. **This permits the rough plumbing to be completed and pressure tested before setting the fixtures.** Then the cabinet work can be completed and the fixtures put in place.

By preparing an isometric drawing similar to the diagram shown below with approximate location of each fixture and element, the number of elbows, tees, crosses and

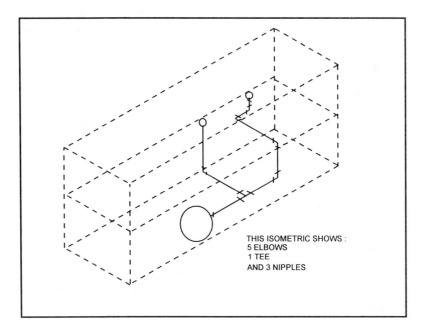

THIS ISOMETRIC SHOWS:
5 ELBOWS
1 TEE
AND 3 NIPPLES

adapters may be counted. Also, the approximate length of piping may be estimated this way. This isometric drawing may be prepared by drawing an elongated box representing the coach, with a middle plane to represent the floor, as shown in the drawing. Note the drawing is an example only, and is purposely left simple for clarity. The location of the fixtures and appliances may be approximated and connected with the piping as needed.

The common plumbing fittings are the elbow to turn corners, the tee, couplings, unions and nipples. The elbows may be ninety degrees, or forty-five degrees. The most common is the standard elbow with female threads at each opening. A street elbow has male threads on one opening and female threads on the other. The tee is used to intersect a line to route the material to another location. A street tee has male threads on one opening and female threads on the other two. A coupling is used to mate or join two lengths of pipe. A union is used to mate two lengths of pipe where there is no room to manipulate the assembly. A nipple is a short length of pipe threaded on both ends. All of these items are available in flanged fittings, but they have no application in this discussion. In addition, fittings are available as compression fittings, and as 45-degree flare type.

Chapter Fourteen

Fixtures

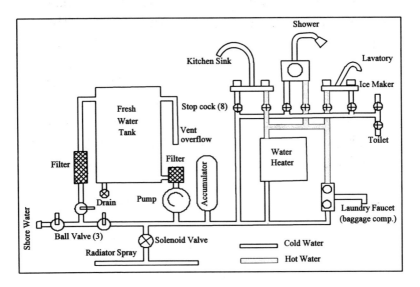

Plumbing fixtures are grouped into two categories: the various plumbing appliances, and the taps or faucets used to serve these appliances. We exclude up-stream valves and stop cocks from the category of faucets.

The kitchen faucet is normally a large swing style spigot, so it may service a double sink. Often this faucet will have a single handle to control; a mixing valve for both hot and cold water. A standard bar sink faucet is formed as a tall curved spigot with individual controls for hot and cold water. A standard lavatory faucet may have a single control or a double, as dictated by decorative considerations. The style of faucets in the areas of the bathroom and kitchen are available in a broad choice of materials, colors and designs, from the bright chrome finish to the gold fixtures with porcelain handles. A utility faucet located in the baggage compartment area is essential, and may be a laundry tub style. It should have a threaded outlet on the spigot so a hose may be connected. It is often useful to connect a hose to a location on the bus conversion for anything from washing a car to adding water to the radiator, or even flushing the holding tank. The most useful purpose of the baggage compartment faucet is for washing hands. Add a paper towel holder for this purpose. The faucet may swing overboard and simply drain on the ground, since it is clean fresh water.

    A critical fixture or appliance is the water heater. Water heaters may be propane (LPG) fired, electrically heated, heated with engine coolant, ie., circulated radiator water, or other heating systems. Some water heaters incorporate all three heating methods. The most efficient heating method is gas fired. It has the fastest recovery time. The common size for a bus conversion water heater is six gallons. This may seem small since most of us have at least a fifty gallon water heater in our homes. These water heaters, however, are very efficient, since six gallons may be reheated very quickly. When you mix six gallons of hot water with six gallons or more of cold water, you have the use of 12 or more gallons of comfortable shower water. This is a long leisurely shower. In fact, a long leisurely shower normally consumes less than eight gallons of water. If you are dry camping these types of showers are to be avoided since you are consuming precious water. A cleansing shower may be had for less than two gallons, or a *Navy bath* with soap, and a wash rag may be accomplished with a quart or two of fresh water. Washing dishes will take less than a gallon of hot water.

Fixtures

LPG water heaters are commonly available in six and ten gallon size. Electric water heaters are available in sizes from ten gallons, twenty gallons and up. Recently, the use of engine coolant for heating bathing and drinking water has been discouraged. In the event of a failure in the system, radiator water with antifreeze may mix with drinking water and could be fatal. And on the other hand, it is another connection. A potential failure point to cause the loss of engine coolant.

Kitchen sinks come in a variety of shape and materials. A common RV sink is stainless steel of a smaller than normal size. Although the sizes may vary a little, 15 inches by 22 inches by a depth of 5 inches is a common small double sink. Since our subject is bus conversions with its associated greater space than an average RV, a standard residential double sink is more appropriate. The standard double sink dimensions are 22" x 32" x 7" depth. They are available in stainless steel, stainless steel undercoated for sound deadening, enameled steel, corian (an acrylic-clay composite), polyester marble and porcelainized cast iron. The sizes cover a broad spectrum. Those listed are simply representative. Holes are provided on the rear flange of sinks to accommodate the faucet soap dispensers and flexible hoses. In addition, a hole may be used for a dishwasher vent, although a dishwasher is not recommended in a conversion because of the high water consumption. If the planned usage of the conversion is exclusive campground parking, a built-in dishwasher may be appropriate. If so, piping should be routed for this purpose.

The shower enclosure may be purchased as a unit or fabricated in place. Again, a broad spectrum of choices are available, ranging from fiberglass stalls with standard doors, to exotic see-through units with curved glass doors. One unit seen a few years ago was a liquid crystal wall which was completely transparent until electrically switched to an opaque mode. If a *fabricate-in-place* shower is desired, it is suggested that a standard fiberglass pan be used. Fabricating the pan in place, unless done by an expert, can result in leakage. The walls of a shower may be done with a high pressure laminate such as Formica, corian, synthetic onyx, a glazed masonite, or even ceramic tile. If tile is used, one method of setting it is with a silicone rubber and grouted with a tub and tile sealer. These materials are flexible and will withstand the moving loads of the vehicle. Although somewhat heavy, the traditional wire mesh and grout base for tile stands up well in a coach due to the torsional rigidity and suspension of the vehicle. Finally, home improvement outlets stock a modern, cement composite board designed to be used as a base for ceramic tile. The shower mixing valve is normally a single knob unit controlling both the temperature and the flow rate.

  The lavatory, also known as the hand basin, may be corian, cultured marble, stainless steel, ceramic or cast iron. Any of these materials will serve adequately. The choice of this fixture is generally a decorator item, and is limited only by taste and cost. Customarily, the lavatory faucet incorporates a stopper for the basin.

  Until recently, a separate ice maker was installed in most conversions. However, double door refrigerators are now available for RV applications with a built-in ice maker. These generally take up an additional eight inches of wall space, whereas the smallest stand alone ice maker uses fourteen inches of wall space, albeit, only half as high. The volume used is similar to the ice maker, but with the added advantage of a freezer compartment and a full height refrigerator. The ice maker needs only a quarter-inch line leading from the stop cock to the unit. Compression fittings are commonly used.

The toilet, like the ice maker, uses only cold water, and a flexible line may connect the unit from the stop cock. Toilets made from plastic bodies are available, but a ceramic porcelain unit is preferred for sanitation. The plastic toilets are relatively inexpensive, and when they fail is it a simple matter to replace them. Toilets are available which use both water and vacuum and are considered the top of the line. Thetford is the primary manufacturer of the plastic style of RV toilet. SeaLand is the principle brand of the porcelain toilet. The top of the line in RV toilets is made by Microphor. The Microphor brand of toilet employs both water and air pressure, or vacuum for its operation.

Since new products are coming along continuously, it would be impossible to adequately cover every feature of every fixture available for a conversion. Keep in mind most residential fixtures are adaptable across the board to conversions. The principle reason residential toilets are not normally used in conversions is they consume a large amount of water for each operation.

The Bus Converter's Bible

Notes:

Sketches

Chapter Fifteen

Waste Water Schematic

This section will discuss the waste water system suggesting alternatives and options that may be incorporated into the design. The debate continues to the separation of the black and grey water (the black water being defined as that waste water generated solely by the toilet; all other sources of waste water defined as grey). Virtually all production motorhomes, and professionally done bus conversions employ both a grey water tank and a black water tank per RVIA standards (see page 14). Although this has become the standard of the industry, as argued in a later chapter, this is a choice that the owner has when doing it his way. Obviously, if you wish to earn the RVIA decal you must comply with their standards.

The waste water piping, like residential usage, is exclusively ABS, although PVC is occasionally seen. The schematic shown in the figure on the next page may be considered a typical design. Obviously, additional fixtures require additional piping, but the design shown may be used as a guide.

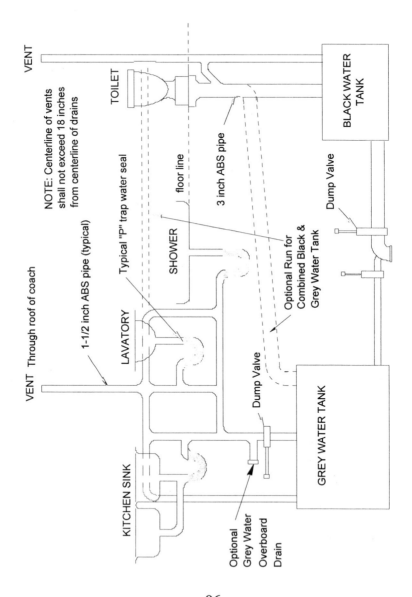

Chapter Sixteen

Black Water Scheme

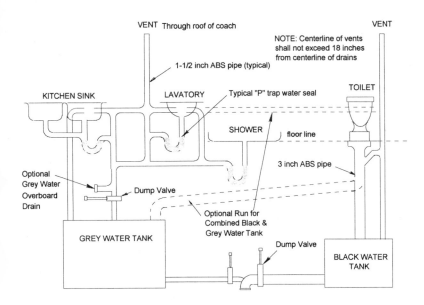

The drawing shown above illustrates two separate holding tanks: one for the grey water and one for the black water. Black water was defined earlier as body waste material that is generated from the toilet. There is no circumstance where black water may be dumped onto the ground. Black water must be dumped into a suitable septic or sewage system.

As with all holding tank systems, the tank must be vented to atmosphere. In addition, it is necessary to provide a vent close to the toilet as shown in the drawing in order to prevent a loss of the water seal and leakage of the sewer gases from the tank into the coach. The black water system must be sized with 3-inch ABS piping and associated dump valves. It may be useful to provide a dump on each side of the coach. Many cases it would be convenient to hook up to a sewer drain, or clean-out, on the right side. Traditionally, the primary dump position is located on the left hand side of the coach, per RVIA standards, and all RV parks provide the utility connections on this side.

Although it is customary to provide both a black water tank and a separate grey water tank, many people prefer to combine the tanks into a single unit for simplicity. The phantom lines on the drawing show this option. If this sort of design is preferred, it is suggested that if the toilet cannot be placed directly over the tank, the fall of the piping must be at least 3/4 inch to the foot. Conventional residential drains, by code, must have a fall of 1/4 inch in a foot, but in the case of a motorcoach conversion the greater drainage slope compensates for some degree out of level.

In the event of a single waste holding tank, the vent piping of the toilet may be coupled with the other vent piping as shown by the phantom lines, so only one vent pipe penetrates the roof of the bus. This vent must be at least a 2-inch pipe. Again, if a single tank is used, consider providing a dump valve on each side of the coach for convenience. Although a curb-side dump is contrary to RVIA standards, it might be construed as a cleanout.

In a standard residential toilet, a water trap is cast integral with the unit. Very few RV or marine toilets are made with water traps. So the logical question is why do we vent the RV toilet? First the RV toilet uses a water seal to insure sewer gases do not invade the coach. Now, due to the motion of the coach, possible gases may be pumped up through the waste piping and go through the water seal, so venting of a black water tank is doubly important. Hence, the design shown is appropriate.

Chapter Seventeen

Grey Water Scheme

Examine each fixture in the figure below, and with the exception of the toilet, you will see a "P" trap follows. The purpose of the "P" trap is to contain a quantity of drain water to form a seal and prevent gases from the holding tank from invading the coach. Adjacent to, or very close to the trap, is a vent. This vent should be no farther than 18 inches from the

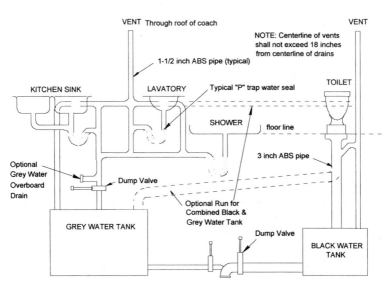

trap. The vents may be brought together, combined into a single stack (minimum pipe size 1¼ inch dia.), then continue through the roof of the coach where the odor is dissipated in the same manner as in residential construction. Without these vents for each fixture, the sewer gases, due to sloshing, or a pumping action due to the coach motion, would penetrate the water seal, hence the coach. Keep in mind, if you are camping for a long time without using a fixture, the trap may evaporate, allowing the noxious gases to enter the living area. This might happen if you are in an RV park where you take showers at the parks facility instead of in the coach. Through lack of use the water in the trap under the shower may evaporate.

Although this is sure to be a controversial subject, a unique feature of this schematic is the *Optional Grey Water Overboard Drain*. Grey water in a few places is considered to be non-polluting and may be drained directly onto the ground. This device would simply be a tee leading to a hose bib connection with a shut-off valve, or dump valve between the connection and the tank. The hose could then be routed to an appropriate drain or sewer. This item would allow grey water to be drained from the coach overboard where permitted, to be re-cycled for gardening or other non-polluting uses. With this option, a coach with an adequate black water tank may be occupied for months without the need to go to a dump station. This feature could be used even if a single waste water holding tank is employed, ie., a combined black-grey water tank. Keep in mind some of these radical suggestions may jeopardize the approval of your coach by the officials. Again, these are the decision the readers must make.

Many people prefer the simplicity and convenience of a single combined black-grey water tank (see admonition, page 95). Only one tank need be monitored, and only one tank need be dumped. With multiple tanks, the content of each must be monitored and each tank fills at a separate rate and requires

Grey Water Scheme

dumping at separate times. Furthermore, with a large single tank located symmetrically and laterally in the coach baggage compartment, it lends itself to installing a dump valve at each side of the coach, increasing the convenience of maneuvering to a sewer clean-out or drain. In addition, this tank may be conveniently located near the center of gravity of the coach, thus maintaining the kinetic trim of the coach.

The discussion in the fresh water section on tankage apply to the waste water holding tanks as well. A multitude of materials are available, but as a practical matter, rotational molded polypropolene is strongly recommended.

Several methods for monitoring the liquid levels in tanks are available. This is especially important in tanks which are hidden by sanitary, professional looking laminate bulkheads. If the tanks are fabricated from opaque materials, it is important to determine their liquid level. In plastic tanks, a common monitor uses stainless steel screw heads as a technique for determining the liquid level. Pairs of screws are inserted in the tank wall with sealing grommets around them. A voltage is sent to one side of these screws where they are immersed in liquid, the resistance is reduced, thereby indicating a specific screw is submerged. These signals are sent to a read out monitor to provide the information as to the approximate liquid level. Another form of monitor for plastic tanks is a pair of foil strips bonded to the outside of the tank walls. These are wired up and as the tanks fills, the capacitance changes, so again a signal is sent to and interpreted and displayed by the monitor. In a metallic tank, a simple float attached to a potentiometer sends a message to a fuel gauge style of readout. This form of gauge is a standard off-the-shelf item. Another form of gauge is a sight gauge, which is nothing but a glass or plastic tube outside of the tank, but connecting the top and bottom of the tank. The level of the liquid will be clearly displayed in the glass. Finally, a new simple gauge is available which is a tube in the bottom of the tank reading the hydrostatic pressure of the liquid in the tank. A water column generates approximately 4.5 pounds per square inch, and so a gauge may be calibrated to indicate the height of the water in a tank.

Chapter Eighteen

Pipe and Fittings

Modern piping used for drain, vent, and waste water is universally ABS, a black plastic pipe which is easily sawn or glued, and flexible enough to yield to a little misalignment. In motor coach application two sizes are commonly used: 1-1/2-inch diameter IPS (iron pipe size) for most applications and vents, and 3-inch for black water applications 3-inch is also used for attachment to the sewer connection.

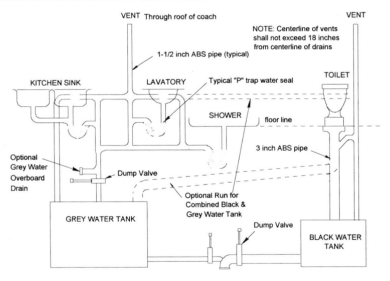

The glue used to attach fittings to ABS pipe is a filled solvent type which, after curing, creates a chemical and mechanical bond as strong as the original pipe. After application to both the male and female surfaces of a joint, the two should be joined within five to ten seconds. A very little adjustment is permitted before the joint becomes immovable. In the event of a mistake, it is best to cut, or saw the mistake out of the system and begin again. The cost of this piping is minimal compared to the old fashioned cast iron sewer pipe with its caulked and leaded joints. In addition, ABS is an ideal material for this application because it's placiticity (low modulus of elasticity, or rubberyness) allows it to perform in a high motion and high vibration environment. Furthermore, ABS is light in weight and adds little weight to a conversion.

In addition to the standard elbows and tees for ABS pipe, special fittings for drain, vent and waste piping are available. Forty-five degree elbows and thirty degree elbows are available. More important, short sweep and long sweep tees are available. The sweep fittings are used to direct the flow of the waste water. By examining the diagram a sweep tee can be seen used just below the right hand kitchen sink bowl, draining from the left hand bowl. Another one can be seen from the "P" trap into the drain. A long sweep elbow would be appropriate from the left hand sink bowl to the sweep tee noted above. An example of a conventional tee would be at the point where the vertical vent ties into the cross-over vent. A simple rule is to use a sweep elbow or tee where you wish to direct the drainage. It would be meaningless to use sweep fittings in pure ventilation applications.

Dump valves are available in 1½-inch and 3-inch sizes. These valves are nothing more than simple slide style gate valves made of plastic which may be bonded or attached with threaded fittings. Furthermore, combination 1½ to 3-inch fittings are available which permits two separate tanks to be joined to a single dump fitting with the two size dump valves on either side. With this sort of fitting, the black water may be dumped. Then the grey water may be dumped and used to partially backflush the black water tank before draining into the dump hose.

The dump hoses are available from RV supply stores with numerous lengths, grades and attach fittings. These hoses are 3-inch diameter spiral wire reinforced vinyl tubing similar to residential dryer vent hoses.

Keep in mind in the design of your drain, vent, and waste system, that each fixture requires a vent pipe and the closer the vent is to the fixture the less chance sewer gases will penetrate into the coach living quarters. A simple venturi may be mounted over the exit of the vent system on the roof of the coach, and will provide a negative pressure in the vent system while the coach is moving. This is useful because the motion of the coach causes some degree of sloshing, or pumping, of these gases and the odors bubbling up through the traps can be very disagreeable. Under normal conditions the water seal in the trap prevents any gases from escaping into the coach, but as mentioned earlier, it is a good idea to check all your traps to see that they are filled with water before moving the coach.

Notes:

Sketches

Chapter Nineteen

Liquid Petroleum Gas

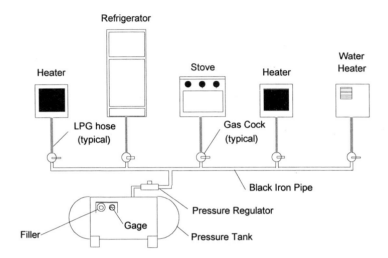

　　Liquid Petroleum Gas (LPG) as a fuel, is considered by many to be avoided in favor of an all-electric coach, and then there are those who are afraid of natural gas in their homes. In terms of economics, LPG is the least expensive form of cooking, heating and refrigeration. In addition, propane is equally as safe as electricity. Each form of energy must be properly designed to insure safety. Perhaps the most important consideration when designing and installing any form of energy supply system for a motor home, is to anticipate and prevent any possibility of chafing the delivery elements, such as wiring, hoses or piping which may occur as a result of the motion of the coach. It is a simple precaution to wrap or slip another oversize hose over a line piercing a potential chafing spot, as shown in the drawing on page 110. Another important consideration when designing for LPG is adequate ventilation. Propane is heavier than air and if a leak occurs, will sink to the lowest level. Tankage, therefore should be installed in the lowest part of the coach, normally the baggage compartment. In addition, the tanks or tank should be enclosed in a separate compartment with air-tight bulkheads, and ventilating holes in the floor of the compartment. A minimum of two holes must add up to 1 square inch for every 7 pounds of propane. As an example, 2 forty pound tanks will require 12 square inches. This could be 2- 2 x 3 inch openings and may be screened over. Venting is also required near the top.

If you have the slightest degree of concern, go to your propane supplier and learn the name of a certified installer. Then employ this company or individual to complete your

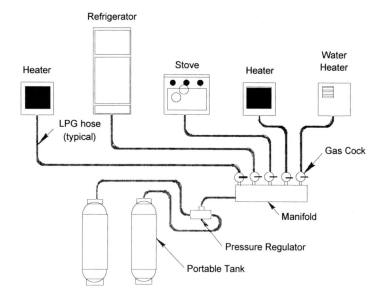

LPG installation. There will then be no question as to whether you have installed your system to the prevailing codes. Hiring an expert is good insurance in an area this important.

Caution should be exercised when the tanks are filled to avoid over-filling. Know the capacity of the tanks and don't let an over zealous salesman give you too much. As a matter of convenience, my preference is to have portable tanks which may be removed from the coach and taken to a filling station for re-fueling. Permanently mounted tanks mean the coach must be driven to a LPG sales point and many times their yard does not lend itself to negotiating the area with a large coach. It is much easier to remove a portable tank from the coach, put it in a car or truck, and drive to the LPG sales yard. In addition, with two portable tanks available, when one tank is exhausted, it is a simple matter to switch to the full tank, remove the empty, and take it to be re-filled. Keep in mind removable tanks must meet the same mounting criteria as permanent tanks; they must be able to withstand a load applied at the center of gravity equal to **eight times** the weight of the filled containers.

When we are on the road, staying no more than a few days at any one location, we leave our refrigerator on LPG exclusively. It is never switched to electricity. We also use LPG for cooking and heating. These conditions are normally in the spring or fall, with a few cold days, cooking in (not going out for dinner, about seventy percent of the time), and full time LPG refrigerator usage. We have found that two ten gallon tanks (also known as forty pound tanks) are adequate to keep us on the road for at least one month. Naturally, as one tank is emptied, it is re-filled.

Most LPG tanks are certified for twelve years and must be re-certified or replaced at the end of this time. A date code stamped on the tank determines it's certification. Some tanks are only certified for four years. Your LPG supplier can inform you as to the certification of your tanks.

These tanks are similar to air pressure tanks, with domed ends. The gas is filled under high pressure so it is a liquid while in the tank. Propane, the most common form of LPG, weighs about four pounds to the gallon, is highly volatile and will remain a liquid only under approximately 130 psi absolute. This value varies considerably with temperature. Butane is a fuel which is used where low volatility is needed, consequently is not normally used for cooking and heating in motorhome applications.

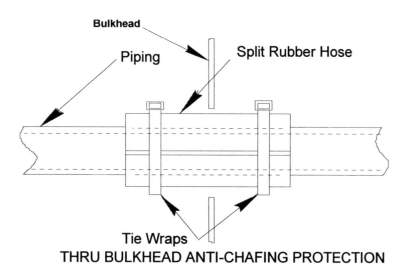

THRU BULKHEAD ANTI-CHAFING PROTECTION

Propane in its natural state is practically odorless, so organic sulphur compounds (a strong garlic smell) are added in order to detect the presence of the gas. The standard is a normal person will be able to detect the presence of the gas

Liquid Petroleum Gas

when the concentration reaches 1 percent of gas in air. The lower limit of flammability of gas is about 5 percent, so the 1 percent requirement is basically one-fifth the lower limit of flammability. The combustion of these lower limits does not create any serious problems. It certainly does, however, alert one to a leak.

Down stream of the storage tank or tanks, is a pressure regulator. This reduces the liquid pressure so it becomes a low pressure gas. The pressure delivered to the appliances is normally about 11 inches of water, or a little over 4 pounds per square inch. A master shut-off valve should be installed between the pressure regulator and the distribution system. Most residential code mandates the use of black iron for piping. Aluminum piping is allowed, but I consider it too fragile for use in a moving vehicle, considering the potential for chafing and vibration. In California, the codes discourage copper in LPG usage because the odorizing material (garlic odor) added to LPG is corrosive to copper. Another material is a hose which is specifically manufactured for LPG materials. **This hose is clearly marked for use with LPG.**

It is customary to run black iron to, or near, the various appliances terminating in a gas cock, a small valve which opens and closes with a ninety degree turn similar to a ball valve. Be sure to use **L-P gas listed shut-off cocks**. Gas cocks and the various appliances generally terminate with a three-eighths inch /forty-five degree flare fitting. From the gas cocks, similar to the stop cocks in water plumbing, a flexible hose with female flare fitting nuts at each end is used to complete the run to the appliance, as shown in the figure page on 107. These hoses are made up with a forty-five degree flare insert, a female coupling nut, and a swedged collar. Again, these hoses must be **LPG listed.**

Another approach to an LPG installation is to fabricate, or purchase a manifold with multiple openings. These are available in aluminum or may be fabricated by drilling holes through a block of aluminum and creating female threads by tapping with a quarter-inch IPS tap, see page 193. The ports not used may simply be plugged with a pipe plug. Gas cocks may then be installed in this manifold with a master shut-off valve installed at one point between delivery hose and the pressure regulator. Each gas cock may be numbered and dedicated to a specific appliance. The rest of the delivery system to the various appliances can then be LPG hoses, as shown in the drawing on page 108. The hoses are more easily routed than the iron pipe, and this design allows all the joints to be concentrated to check for leaks. After completing the hook-up, the pressure tight integrity is checked by pressurizing with air, then spraying a soapy solution at each connection. This immediately displays a leak in the form of a soap bubble, and appropriate action may then be taken.

Part Three

Electrical Systems

The Bus Converter's Bible

Chapter Twenty

Power Requirements

We first must define the term *power*. The expression voltage in electrical terms is likened to electrical pressure, as in water pressure. The expression amperes is defined as the amount of electrical current, or flow rate. And power is the product of the two expressed in watts, and may be equated to the volume of usage. Our electrical bills reflect the volume of electricity we use in kilowatt-hours. Today our residential power costs us about ten to fifteen cents per kilowatt-hour.

Power is always the same whether we are using 12VDC, 120VAC, or 440V single phase or three-phase, and is defined as the product of voltage times amperes. If we use the symbol "**E**" for voltage, (Electromotive force), and "**I**" for the amperes (Induced current) and "**P**" for power, the equation **P=EI** is the universal definition of power. The equation may be rewritten as Amperage equals wattage divided by voltage (**I=P÷E**).

So if an appliance draws 1200 watts at 120 volts alternating current, we can see by dividing the voltage into the wattage (1200÷120=10), the amperage is 10. In another example, if an appliance draws 600 watts in a 12 volt direct current application, the current used is 600÷12=50 amps. This indicates it does not matter whether the electrical source is alternating current or direct current, the amount of current is only a factor of the power and voltage. This concept becomes very important when we analyze our battery requirements.

In every case the definition of power is expressed in terms of one hours worth of usage. This means in the examples above, the 1200 watt appliance uses 10 amps per hour while running, and the other unit uses 50 amps per hour while it is cycling. Even though one unit uses alternating current and the other uses direct current, except for some minor efficiency factors the two currents may be equated. We will leave this discussion temporarily while we explore the total power requirements of a motor coach.

To determine the power requirements for a coach, all we have to do is add up the wattage of each electrical devise on board. To begin with, one horsepower equals 745 watts, but for conservative simplicity we use 1000 watts, or 1 kilowatt per horsepower. So, it is a simple matter to examine all the devices with an electrical motor and add the horsepower and convert to kilowatts. The most power hungry items of equipment are the air conditioning units. Each ton of air conditioning is 12,000 BTU, and consumes about 12 amperes at 120 volts, or about 1.5 kilowatts. An average electrical water heater uses a 1.5 kilowatt heating element. The average television uses about 200 watts. A toaster is 1200 watts, a hair dryer is 1200 watts, and a microwave oven is about 700 watts. A four foot florescent tube is 40 watts while an eight foot florescent tube is 75 watts.

Almost all electrical devises with a UL rating (Underwriters Laboratory) will list on a placard mounted on the unit the power consumption. All that is necessary is we add up all the wattage of every electrical item, including light bulbs, and we have our total wattage needs. Now it is obvious every piece of electrical equipment in a coach will not be on simultaneously, but in case this happens, we size our power requirements to this unlikely event. The example given below is typical of an average motorcoach conversion:

Power Requirements

Device	Wattage
Air Conditioners (2 @ 1,500)	3,000
Water Heater	1,500
Microwave	750
Toaster	1,200
Hair dryer	1,000
Lamps (10 @ 75)	750
Refrigerator	500
Televisions (2 @ 200)	400
Computer	<u>250</u>
Total	**9,350**

The figure shown is only a little under 10 kilowatts, which means the minimum size generator must be a ten KW unit if all the appliance operated simultaneously. With the above requirements, an eight kilowatt generator should certainly be adequate since it is unlikely that all the appliances would be on at the same time. This decision, however, must be made by the user.

The table below shows the ampere draw as a function of the wattage and the voltage.

	Ampere Draw			
Wattage	12 V	24 V	120 V	240 V
100	8.4	4.2	0.84	0.42
200	16.7	8.4	1.7	0.84
300	25	12.5	2.5	1.3
400	34	16.7	3.4	1.7

500	41.7	21	4.2	2.1
1000	84	42	8.4	4.2
1500	125	63	12.5	**6.3**
2000	167	84	16.7	8.4
2500	209	105	21	10.5

This table points out another interesting fact. Since an appliance is designed to draw a specific wattage, and the wiring in this appliance is sized for a specific ampere draw at a specific voltage, it must be understood that a lower voltage will cause a higher ampere draw, thus overheating the appliance. This may cause a failure of the unit. On the other hand, a voltage that is too high could cause over-speeding of the appliance which is also detrimental. So it is important to match the proper voltage to the proper appliance.

Chapter Twenty One

Battery Requirements

In the example in the previous chapter, we determined we needed a ten kilowatt power source. Disregarding the voltage at this point, we must now determine our battery bank to support ten kilowatts of need.

Batteries are rated in amp-hours. This is the number of amperes stored, times the number of hours of life. As an example, a 220 amp-hour battery can store and deliver 22 amps for ten hours, or 2.2 amps for 100 hours, or 220 amps for one hour. These values are under ideal conditions, and should be discounted approximately fifty percent for voltage drop. They are useful, however, as a guide.

The first assumption we make is we will not permit the very high power requirements to draw on the battery bank through the inverter (see Chapter 23). Specifically, we should not try to run our air conditioners with battery power. If we did, we would soon find our battery bank exhausted, or we would need such a bank of batteries the coach may be too heavy to move. Let us decide, however, that we must power our refrigerator, our cook top, and our water heater with electricity converted to AC through an inverter. These items represent a very high drain on our batteries.

Let us assume the water heater cycle turns on for ten minutes, every two hours, except when some one is using the shower. Each time it cycles, its power consumption is 1500 watts times ten minutes. This is one-sixth of an hour times 1500, and equals 250 watts. Assuming it cycles 15 times a day, it will demand nearly 4000 watts. Divide this by 12 volts and you will need over 300 amp-hours of battery capacity to operate a water heater for one day.

A microwave oven using 750 watts for six minutes (one-tenth of an hour) will consume 75 watts divided by 12 volts which is a little over 6 amp-hours. A 1200 watt toaster on for 3 minutes only uses 5 amp-hours. A 240 watt television on for three hours will use 60 amp-hours. An average residential refrigerator will use about 200 amp-hours per day. An electrical cook-top used to prepare meals for about 30 minutes twice a day will use about 200 to 300 amp-hours. Finally, other normal electrical items such as lighting will use about 50 to 70 amp-hours per day.

Adding up the usage outlined above, we find we need a battery bank with about 800 amp-hours per day. This size of the battery bank could be achieved with four 220 amp-hours batteries. Assuming we have a means of recharging our batteries at the rate of 200 amperes per hour, it would be necessary to recharge for four (4) hours per day. (Note: if the batteries were charged at 200 amps, they would probably explode, or melt.) If we wish to go more than a day without recharging the batteries, we simply install a larger battery bank, and plan to recharge them for a longer time.

From the above example, the advantage of propane for space heating, water heating, refrigeration and cooking is obvious. Removing these items from our list of power-hungry equipment, a new assessment reveals an eight-hundred amp-hour battery bank would allow us to last over a week without recharging our batteries. However, if we are in a traveling mode, as opposed to simply being parked, our engine driven alternator could be switched to charge our house batteries while going down the road to satisfy even the most severe conditions.

Battery Requirements

To re-cap, let us describe a scenario whereby we run our refrigerator on propane, our water heater on propane, and we cook and heat with propane. The weather is mild, so air conditioning is not needed. We have found a delightful spot near a running stream, and have left our cares at the office. First thing each morning we make coffee. It takes six minutes to drip through making three full mugs. We have either toast or frozen waffles from the toaster taking three minutes. Our day is spent reading, fishing, hiking, and just sitting, enjoying the peace and beauty of our location. For lunch we heated up some frozen sandwiches in the microwave oven (this is also a vacation for your bride, remember?). This took six minutes for both sandwiches. Later that evening, we had a frozen desert from the microwave, another six minutes. That night, we enjoyed a movie we brought along in the form of a video tape, for a little over two hours. After her shower, your wife dried her hair with the hair dryer for nine minutes. How many kilowatts did we use, and more important, how many amps did we withdraw from the (battery) bank?

Coffee (1200 watt x .1 hour) . . . . 120.
Toast or Waffles (1200 watt x 0.05 hours) 60.
M/W Sandwiches (720 watt x 0.20 hours) 144.
Video Tape Player (120 watt x 2 hours)   240.
Television (180 watt x 2 hours) . . . . 360.
Hair Dryer (900 watt x 0.15 hours) . . . . 135.
Utility lighting . . . . 250.
Total watts used = ... **1309.**

With a 12-volt battery bank, you used 1309÷12 =109 amperes, or with a 24-volt battery bank you used about 55 amperes. These figures assume you have an inverter with 100 percent efficiency. In the real world, with losses to heat and other intangibles, you probably used about 120 amps from a 12-volt battery bank. Determine the number of days you would like to repeat this idyllic existence, and size your battery bank accordingly.

Chapter Twenty Two

Generators

Recalling our discussion of power requirements in chapter twenty, the size of the generator should be large enough to satisfy the demands of every appliance in the coach including their start-up load factor. Start-up load factors are not relevant in heating type devices such as lamps, heaters and televisions. Start-up factors should be considered with any type of rotating machinery, such as motors and air conditioners. Although these factors vary with the type of motor and the load conditions, it is important to use a load factor ranging from 5 to 7 on these applications. Even the modern rotary air conditioners with a running load of 15 amps need about 80 amps to start.

Generators may be set to provide either 240-volt alternating current, or 120-volt AC. This is a preference to be made by the owner. By selecting the 240VAC option, two 120-volt legs may be run to the distribution panel, but the problem of balancing the loads must be solved. The advantages of the 240-volt option is one leg may be dedicated to relatively small loads for convenience, such as lighting and entertainment. This leg may then also be supplied by an inverter powered by the battery bank to provide electrical conveniences while the generator is not running. In balancing the load with a 240-volt system, it is obvious if two air conditioning units are used, each one should be supplied by each leg. One drawback with the inverter dedicated to one leg and an air conditioner also running on that leg is, if the generator were to shut down, the inverter would try to run the A/C depleting the batteries and damage the A/C. Other high load appliances should be as evenly shared by the two legs as possible. Another advantage to the 240 volt system, is the capability of operating high voltage equipment, such as an electric cooktop, or a welder directly from the generator. As far as hooking up to shore power where only low voltage is available, the land line, or umbilical simply plugs into an adapter feeding both legs with a single hot lead. These adapters are available in RV supply stores. However, it must be cautioned, with this system 240-volt appliances could not be operated. In order to design for 240-volt appliances, a hot lead is employed from each leg, and the shore line must be plugged into a 240-volt source, a convenience not available in every trailer park.

Without a doubt, the simplest way to set up the generator is 120-volt AC. With this approach, there is no need to balance the load distribution. The inverter(s) may then serve a selected group of appliances through a sub-panel. The battery bank delivering power to the inverter, however, must be capable of supplying all the electrical demands of this sub panel. If the battery bank is too small to achieve these demands, it is mandatory the inverter be able to be switched out of the system in the event the generator is providing power, but fails for some reason. If this were to happen, the battery bank would be depleted in short order.

Generators are available in gasoline, propane, or diesel power. Since our conversions are primarily powered with diesel fuel, it is logical to select a diesel powered generator. Many conversions do use both diesel and propane. Although propane does not have the efficiency that diesel fuel has, it is an extremely clean burning, non-polluting fuel. In addition, propane fueled motors remain exceptionally clean.

If a diesel fueled generator is selected because it is the common fuel of the primary coach engine, it is important not to simply "tee-off" from the coach fuel line. The coach engine pump moves well over sixty gallons of fuel per hour. This would probably starve the generator if an attempt were made to run them simultaneously. So, it is imperative a separate fuel line and return fuel line be dedicated to the generator.

The generator should be mounted in a clean compartment with a flow of fresh air available. This fresh air may be achieved by installing a blower or fan. The radiator for the generator may be remotely mounted, as long as it too has a supply of clean, fresh, cool air. For example, it would not be wise to mount the generator radiator in the coach engine compartment where it would be subject to the hot air radiating from the motor. A logical location would be a baggage compartment behind the forward axle bulkhead, where a source of cooling air may be obtained between the steering tires. Another common acceptable practice is to connect the generator cooling system into the coach cooling system. This has the advantage the coach engine temperature gauges also reflect the temperature of the generator engine.

It is recommended the generator be mounted in a frame or cage which may be rolled out or swung out in order to simplify maintenance. A typical swing-out mount is described in chapter nine. Since the average ten kilowatt diesel generator weighs less than 500 pounds, a simple frame with a torsion bar along the hinge line will provide adequate support with almost no detectable deflection, or sag.. The muffler system for the generator may be included within the sliding or swing mount. It is recommended the exhaust from the generator be directed to a remote location while parked next to other coaches. An ideal solution would be to direct the exhaust through the roof of the coach. This may be done by routing the exhaust pipe through a slightly larger section of transite, cement pipe, or other form of insulating conduit.

The wiring leading from the generator to the distribution panel must be sized according to the current carried. As was mentioned in the introduction, a smattering of Ohm's Law would be presented. This law is simply **E=IR**, and means **E**, the electromotive force (commonly called **voltage**) is equal to the product of the

current I and the **resistance R**. The larger the wire, the less resistance it has, hence a greater current may flow through that wire at a given voltage. We will select either 120 volts, or 240 volts, so in this respect, the voltage for our application is fixed. The table below is a listing of the acceptable current values for two types of copper wire size with less than a 50 foot run as suggested by the Uniform Building Code.

Gauge	Standard Insulation	High Temperature
14	15 amps	22 amps
12	20 amps	27 amps
10	25 amps	37 amps
8	35 amps	49 amps
6	45 amps	65 amps
4	60 amps	86 amps
2	80 amps	115 amps

To determine the wire size from a generator to the distribution panel, divide the wattage by the voltage to find amps, and then read the wire size from the table above. Using a ten kilowatt generator with a simple 120-volt system, 10,000 watts ÷ 120-volts = 83.34 amperes. This suggests the wire size should be number 4 high temperature. If we wish to use a 240-volt system, then 10,000 watts ÷ 240-volts = 41.67 amperes. In this case, we could use either number 6 standard, or number 8 high temperature wire.

A small editorial note might be appropriate at this point. Commonly we hear house voltage referred to as 110 volts, or 115 volts, or even 117 volts. And, we often hear the higher voltage referred to as 220. Voltage is derived as a result of the division of the transmission of very high voltage. Although the value of the transmitted voltage varies according to the distance and the

terrain, one of the more common transmission voltages is 12,000 volts. Step down transformers are then employed to divide this transmitted voltage down to 480 volts, and 240 volts. Almost all voltage delivered to a residence through a step down transformer is 240 volts. Appliance makers often refer to a design operating voltage of 117. This is to compensate for voltage drops as a result of normal line loss due to conductor resistance. At anytime, a meter may be applied to a wall outlet in a house and the voltage will fluctuate from about 108 on the low side to as high as 124. These fluctuations are caused by a myriad of reasons, from public demand to sun spots. As is obvious from the discussion above, I prefer to stick to the simplicity of multiples of 120. The principle advantage this has, it is easily divisible by the most common direct current voltage, ie., 12 and 24 volts.

One very important accessory for the generator should be considered. This is an automatic start device that may be added for about ten percent additional cost to the generator. This automatic start system may be triggered by several options. One option built into the system is a low battery condition. This will sense a low battery bank, turn on your generator, re-charge your batteries to specific level then shut itself off. The low battery sensor is designed to sample your voltage over a time period so it will not start the generator simply because of a transitory condition. Another form of sensor samples the outside temperature. This sensor may set for a low temperature so your generator may turn on and drive electric heaters to warm your coach, or to sense a high temperature so that your air conditioning may be powered on automatically. Obviously, manual controls are built in so you may turn off this feature if you don't want it operable while you are sleeping. This accessory has a built in alarm buzzer warning anyone in near proximity it is about to start. Finally, the number of start attempts may be adjusted, since sometimes motors do not start on the first try. This can be set for maximum reliability.

Chapter Twenty Three

Converters, Inverters, and Chargers

We will now clarify several of the confusing terms listed in this chapter heading. Converters, inverters, and chargers may all include a battery charging system.

A converter is basically a device which converts alternating current, like standard residential current to direct current through a *rectifier*. A *rectifier* is basically a large step down transformer with diodes, or electrical check valves which force the alternating current to emerge as a directional one way current. This permits the converter to act like a battery charger. In addition, a converter will have a series of fuse holders so a direct current system of circuits may be distributed throughout the coach. Converters are not as often seen with the advance of solid state devices.

An inverter is an electrical device which does the opposite of a converter. It takes direct current and changes it to alternating current, such as we have in our houses. The earlier inverters were direct current motors driving an alternator. The most common unit was made by Honeywell, known as a Readyline. Readyline, and Powerline are trademarks of Honeywell. These units were available in 500, 1000 and 1500 watts. No doubt larger sizes were available, but not as common. The principle problem with the motor driven inverters was the high overhead in battery power needed to operate them. For example, a 1000-watt unit could run a television which used only 120 watts, but instead of drawing 10 amps from the battery bank, it would draw over 15 amps. This was because a minimum power drain was used to simply turn the rotor. This results in a poor efficiency rating of the rotating style of the inverter; on the order of 55 to 70 percent. Additionally, the rotating inverter has as whine which can get on your nerves if you are sensitive to noise. Quite a few drawbacks, but in the earlier days, it was the only game in town.

The solid state inverter has been around for a number of years, but the earlier ones also had a relatively poor efficiency rating. Tripp is a brand name which comes to mind. The earlier solid state inverters also had an annoying hum, or buzz. In recent years, we have seen the development of the computerized solid state inverters with no moving parts. These units are made by Trace, Best, Heart and no doubt others. These companies have most aggressively entered the RV market. The units are commonly available in 2,000, 2,500, and 5,000 watts. For greater power requirements they may be stacked, or cascaded. This means they may be installed so that their power capabilities are added together to provide all the power a coach needs. In addition, a common inverter option is a built-in battery charger. With the addition of a simple fuse holder for direct current applications, the need for a converter disappears. Another option instead of a fuse holder is a bank of re-settable circuit breakers for direct current applications. Inverters have other options such as remote read-out panels, and remote on/off controls. The read-out panels will display such information as the battery voltage, charging rate in amps, the peak to peak input voltage, and the frequency of the alternating current. The frequency read-out feature is especially useful when setting the speed of the generator drive engine, in the event you receive your generator in an uncalibrated condition or in case the generator motor has to be repaired.

Battery chargers are an essential piece of equipment. They are simply a source of direct current connected in parallel with the battery system. A battery charger is generally set to provide a direct current at 13.8 volts. This value permits the batteries to re-charge, but not boil out the battery acid. In many respects storage batteries may be equated to pails of power, similar to buckets of water. If two batteries were placed side by side with different charges and were connected, the higher charge would pour over into the lesser charge. After a time their charges would be equal. This is similar to *water seeking its own level*. In a simplified manner, this is basically what a battery charger does. A bank of batteries whose reading may be 12.3 volts, when connected to a 13.8 volt charging system will, ultimately, come up to 13.8 volts over a period of time. The charger will begin by charging at a high rate, but will, as the voltage builds up in the batteries, taper down to a trickle, hence the term *trickle charge*.

A very sophisticated form of charger is now available for a fairly high cost. This is a marine pulse charger. A unit rated at only 20 amps can cost over $400. A pulse charger is a unique concept in that it has been determined a storage battery would prefer to accept replenishing charges in small doses, instead of a continuous flow. These pulse chargers have been known to restore a depleted battery which has been judged ready for the scrap heap.

Another interesting form of battery charger is the photovoltaic cell or group of cells known as solar panels. This is the passive charging system. Many of us are familiar with the LED, (light emitting diode), a small device that lights up when a voltage is impressed across it. The photovoltaic cell is the opposite of the LED. If a light is shone on the photovoltaic cell, it will yield a voltage. A large array of these cells are combined together to form a solar panel. Solar panels are available in many voltages and power combinations. In the very early days of the solar panel, they were selling for about three dollars per watt; very expensive even by today's standard. It was predicted then the price of the solar panel would ultimately descend to about thirty cents a watt. Because of manufacturing difficulties and a monopoly this never happened and the price of solar panels is still quite high. For approximately 400 plus dollars, however, solar panels may be mounted on the roof of a conversion to provide a battery charging capability from the sun, or even a street lamp. Since many of the solar panels are designed to put out about 18 volts, a voltage regulator is necessary. The voltage of a solar panel is not a constant thing because of the varying intensity of the impinging light. Obviously, on a bright sunny day with the sun nearly overhead, more voltage will be generated than on a dull overcast day with the late afternoon sun.

Wind generators have been available for many years, but I know of no practical unit available for the RV industry. I recall a small wind driven generator to light a lamp on my bicycle which I had as a kid.

Finally, the most common form of battery charger is the motor driven alternator mounted on the primary engine. The more modern units have built-in regulator/rectifying diodes so a voltage regulator is becoming a thing of the past. These are used primarily to maintain the starting batteries, and provide power for the lighting, and automotive accessories. However, a simple circuit will be described in a later chapter so the alternator charges the house batteries as you travel down the road.

Chapter Twenty Four

Fittings and Materials

This chapter will be devoted to common electrical fittings and equipment. These are the items of hardware with which every electrician is familiar, ie., everyday electrical devices for use in residential applications.

All electrical sources should terminate at an electrical distribution panel. This means the shore power, generator power, and inverter power should come to a single point from which, the electricity is then distributed to specific uses.

There is one specialized item of equipment for conversion usage often inserted between the shore power, and/or generator power, before sending it on to the distribution panel. This is an automatic change-over box. This box functions as a sensor of power sources and automatically sends the correct source to the panel. For example, if the generator is started, this box will activate a time delay circuit, allowing the generator to come up to speed and frequency, then snap the power into the panel. Furthermore, if the coach is plugged into shore power and the generator is turned on, it will not permit the generator power to be delivered to the panel. Conversely, if the generator is running, and shore power is inadvertently plugged in, it will again block out the generator giving priority to shore power. In effect, it prioritized the sources of power. This piece of equipment is available from Wrico International of Eugene, Oregon.

The distribution panel is nothing more than the ordinary panel we find in a residential application. The distribution panel is an electrical box containing a collection of circuit breakers. From these breakers, power is routed to the various locations and functions. A special panel is available for conversion usage including both alternating current circuit breakers and a selection of direct current circuit breakers. This item is currently available from Todd Engineering, Elkhart, IN.

The common conductor, or wire, used in residential applications, is Romex. This is a form of two, three, or four wire conductor with a ground wire in a common sheath, or insulation, which may be strung through the interior of residential walls to various locations. In virtually every case these conductors terminate in electrical boxes, and are connected with wire nuts, small fittings that will hand screw onto a pair of twisted wires. Romex, is always composed of solid conductor wire. Although, I have seen Romex used in bus conversions, it not recommended since solid copper tends to work-harden and become very brittle under vibrating loads, hence the risk of breaking. Solid copper wire is not recommended in any moving vehicle application because of the danger of fracture. Furthermore, due to movement, connections tend to loosen causing bad connections and hazards.

All conductors in a coach should be of the fine stranded wire type. Stranded wire is available in both coarse (few strands), and fine (many strands). The coarse strand wire conductor is preferable to solid wire, and is acceptable in this application. The fine stranded wire is the best available.

Another form of wiring available is boat cable. This is the best available. Boat cable is similar to Romex in that it is a multiple conductor cable, but is composed of fine stranded wire that is fully tinned for soldering. In addition, unlike in Romex, the ground wire in boat cable is fully insulated. Boat cable is clearly identified with the printing (WIRE SIZE) BOAT CABLE 600 VOLTS 105°C DRY 75°WET.

The size of wiring in a coach can range from 24 gage signal wire up to four ought, (0000). The determining factor for wire size

Fittings and Materials

is the a combination of current carrying demands and voltage drop. Each appliance or motor demands a certain level of wattage to function. If the voltage is low, the amperes go up to compensate. Remember Ohm's Law, Power (wattage)=Voltage times Amperes? Electrical devices are stupid. When they sense a voltage, they try to operate. If a piece of equipment operates normally at 115 volts and 5 amps, it uses 575 watts. If it senses an 85-volt source, it will still try to work, but will demand almost 7 amps, and since it is designed to use only 5 amps, after a period of time it will likely burn itself out.

The most common wire sizes in a residence is number 12-gage. This is about one-eighth of an inch in diameter. Most convenience outlets are designed for 15 amps, allowing the use of 14-gage conductor, but for simplicity, number 12 is common since it will supply most needs with very little voltage drop. The use of higher voltage, such as 240 volts will allow a smaller wire to be used. To prove this assertion, re-examine the equation above. As mentioned previously wire size is a function of the ampere requirement, and the voltage drop. Voltage drop is not only a function of the wire size, but the wire material and the length of the run. In most respects, we may ignore the length of the run, since we are limited by the size of the coach. If you choose copper as your conductor material, use the table on page 126 to determine wire size.

All conductors should terminate in an electrical box. Since we recommend using stranded wire, the common wire nut is not applicable. All wire connections should be made with a swaging tool, such as the popular *Stakon* brand, or by soldering. This means each end of a wire, regardless of its function should end in a terminal fitting. These terminal fittings may be forks, spades, eyes, or female receptacles. In addition, all wiring should be fastened to permanent structure with wire ties, clamps, grommets, or other means so there is no possibility of wire movement in the coach. Wiring should be protected with metal shields anywhere it could be penetrated by a drill or a screw.

Many circuits terminate at a convenience duplex outlet, or a wall socket. These are generally located in convenient locations, hence the term convenience outlet. These are used to plug lamps, dryers, TVs, razors, and other electrical gadgets, into. Most appliances are plugged into outlets, but occasionally a device is hard wired to a circuit. Generally, roof air conditioners are hard wired to their own circuit. This means from a circuit breaker, normally 30 amps, a set of conductors leads directly to the air conditioner wiring box, and is connected to the internal wiring system of the unit.

Electrical switches come in a variety of designs and applications. The most common are the wall switches in our homes. Most are simply double-pole single-throw switches. They have the ability to connect simultaneously the hot lead and the common lead to the appliance. High current switches are called contactors, or motor starters, and are normally operated with solenoids. Remote switches operated with solenoids are called relays which operate on a low voltage and send a signal to a switch of higher capacity. A common application of a relay is the light switch in our automobiles, operated by a light duty switch on our instrument panel.

Circuit breakers are basically nothing more than a re-settable switch which trips open when it experiences a temperature level over its design value. Most modern circuit breakers in automotive applications will automatically reset, unlike our tripped breakers at home that require us to go to the panel, look for the tripped breaker and manually reset it. All the automotive circuit breaker needs is time to cool down and it will reset itself. Fuses, which are a thing of the past in residential applications,

Fittings and Materials

are still in common usage in automotive circuits. Fuses, by their nature, destroy themselves as they operate and must be replaced. A burned fuse is a signal a problem exists in the vehicle. This should be corrected before installing a larger fuse, or wiring around and defeating the fuse system.

The Bus Converter's Bible

Notes:

Sketches

Chapter Twenty Five

Electrical Circuits

Now we get to the fun part of this book. This is where we create ways to make things happen. This is one area of this book which may reach obsolescence before the rest.

What is an electrical circuit? An electrical circuit can be a simple as an extension cord from a wall outlet to an appliance. If we add an in-line switch, we have added some complexity to our simple circuit. If we add an in-line circuit breaker to limit the amount of current drawn, we have added a little more sophistication to our circuit. Basically, a circuit is nothing more than a road along which the electricity may travel to accomplish a specific job. A circuit diagram is a road map describing this route.

In electrical circuitry, we use two forms of routes; series routing and parallel routing. If the source of power went from one user to the next, giving up a little strength at each user, then on to the next, this would be a series circuit. And, if the wiring was directed from one positive battery terminal to the negative terminal of the next, thereby adding the voltages, this too, is a series circuit.

A description of a standard form of parallel circuitry would be a circuit where we run a bus bar from which we periodically take off to feed an appliance. In electrical circuitry, there is no significant voltage drop in parallel circuits, whereas in series circuits, we experience a drop in voltage from one device to the next. The majority of electrical circuitry is parallel.

Direct current circuits are very simple to understand. In a direct current circuit, the current moves in only one direction;

from the positive anode of the battery, or power source, through the electrical equipment to ground. Almost any convenient location on the frame of the vehicle will serve as ground. The ground must be securely fastened to the frame. A loose ground wire is the most common cause of a direct current circuit failure .

As everyone knows, our automotive batteries get their charge from the engine driven alternator. Our house batteries are generally hooked up to a converter, battery charger, or an inverter, (which switches to a charger when sensing an outside source of 120 VAC). You certainly don't want your two battery systems tied together when dry camping in the event all your DC power was depleted. However, it is desirable to have them tied together when either battery system is being charged. The simple little circuitry shown below will solve the problem.

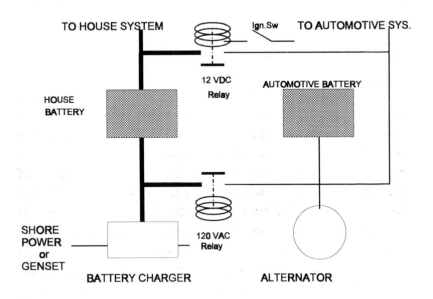

Electrical Circuits

Most of the circuitry shown is direct current, so if you wish you could equate the rectangular figures designated as batteries, to the positive terminal. By examining the circuit, it can be seen that the two systems are completely isolated from each other. When the house battery charger is working from either shore power or the generator, we use the 120-Volt AC source to operate a 120-VAC Relay, which connects the automotive battery system, hence all batteries are being charged. While traveling down the road, a 12-Volt DC relay energized from the ignition switch connects the house battery system to the alternator, so all batteries are being charged.

As to the size of the relays, 100 amp capacities should be sufficient, and number 4 stranded wire is adequate to tie the two systems together. In addition, a third battery, dedicated only to starting the generator, is recommended. So, if all else fails, the generator may be started to charge the starting batteries to get going. Although it is not shown on the diagram, it is advised to mount a 25-amp isolator between the automotive batteries and the small generator battery, so the battery dedicated to the generator is used for no other purpose.

Circuits may be as exotic as you wish. One rather neat idea is a series of circuits whereby you can turn on, or off, a number of conveniences from a number of different locations. Let us examine the following scenario: You have returned from dinner at a restaurant and open your coach. At the entry door is a bank of switches. You are able to turn on the living room light, the bathroom light, the bedroom light, and the CD player. You leave the courtesy light over the front door on, since you are expecting some friends over for cards. Later, your friends leave. You turn off the courtesy light from the living room area, and you also turn off the CD player, but turn on the TV in the bedroom. After getting ready for bed, from the bathroom you turn off the living room lights.

After getting into bed you turn off the bathroom light and the bedroom light. You watch TV for a little while, switch on your security system, turn off the TV from your bedside and go to sleep.

The system just described may have a bank of illuminated push button switches at the entry door, the living room, the kitchen, the dining area, the bathroom, and the bedroom. Any device or appliance can be controlled from any location. This is customarily done with a series of latching relay circuits. A relay known as a bi-stable latching relay causes the contactors to go back and forth from on to off each time you send a current to it, These relays are miniature with a very small current capability and may be used to control the coil of a larger relay. They are known as pilot relays. Latching relays are also available with significant current carrying capability. The advantage of the pilot relay is the wire size may be tiny signal wire. With this type of circuit, all the switches are wired in parallel with the relay, hence the ability to control a single device from multiple sources.

Earlier, we mentioned the simplicity of direct current circuits. Alternating circuits are almost as simple, except the current reverses sixty times per second and it must have a path to follow other than ground. This alternate path is the neutral wire, or common. Each alternating current circuit will have a hot lead, customarily a black wire. The neutral wire is customarily white, and is also known as the common wire. All the common, or neutral, (white) leads in a group of AC circuits may be joined together. Each of the hot leads are a separate circuit and begin from their own breaker. They are then routed to their various usage points. When the power is brought into the distribution panel box, the neutral power wire is attached to a bus bar. The positive wire or wires are attached to bus bar(s) with mounting positions for circuit breakers. It is from these breakers each circuit begins .

The circuitry shown on the next page is a quasi 120/240 volt

Electrical Circuits

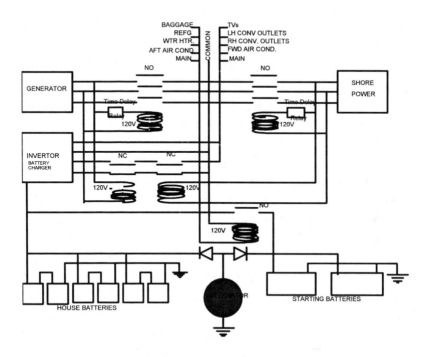

circuit. The generator is set up to produce 240-volt power, but all the circuits in the system are only 120-volt. In this design, the inverter, being driven by the battery bank, delivers 120-volt AC to the right hand side of the distribution panel. In the event either generator or shore power is sensed, the inverter power is disconnected by the normally closed relays in series with the inverter to the panel. Furthermore, the generator, or the shore power returns alternating current to the inverter's battery charging system. Also each source of alternating current goes through a time delay relay circuit before sending the AC to the panel. The motor driven alternator, when running, goes through a set of diodes (an electrical check valve), providing charging power to the batteries. Although the previous circuit is automatic, a simple Murphy-proof circuit is simply an electrical plug which unplugs from the generator source and plugs into a shore power source. This is a manual operation, but has the safety of being fool proof. The same procedure could be followed in the case of an inverter. Keep in mind that automatic devices sometimes fail.

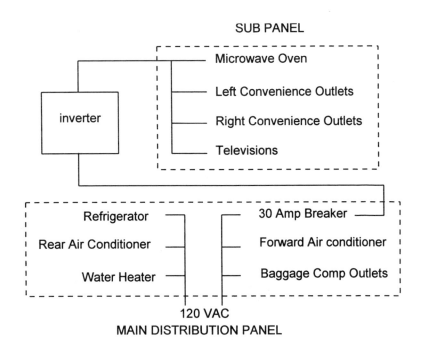

The simple circuit shown above illustrates the design of a sub-panel where the inverter supplies AC only to those appliances within its capacity. The DC power to the inverter is not shown for simplicity. With this design, unlike the previous concept, the inverter will not try to start an air conditioner.

Electrical Circuits

For those of you concerned with 20 or 30 year old wiring in your bus, the diagram on the following pages is the basic 12 VDC automotive wiring needed for a coach without the passenger amenities and the items needed for a public transportation bus. Using this circuitry, you may safely rip and tear out all antique wiring which came with your coach and replace it with new and sanitary circuitry. As a suggestion, however, save all the wire you remove, since it is the best money could buy back then, and probably hasn't improved much in 20 or 30 years.

The wires are identified with simple numbers. The circuit breakers are the little rectangular boxes with a number inside. The upper half of the left hand side of the diagram shows those items which will operate only if the ignition switch is on. Almost any device may be protected with the ignition switch, although there are some items you may wish to operate without having to switch on the ignition .

All of the circuit breakers are 15 amp capacity, and reset automatically. All of the relays are universal. They have two terminals for the coil, one for the common, one normally on, and one normally off. These little relays are about one-inch cubed with spade terminals, are rated at 25 amps, and cost about ten dollars each.

Despite the long runs in a bus, that is from the front to the back, number 14 wire is adequate since all the circuits are 15 amps, or less, . The wire used should be the fine stranded, so that no failure due to vibration fatigue will occur.

The Bus Converter's Bible

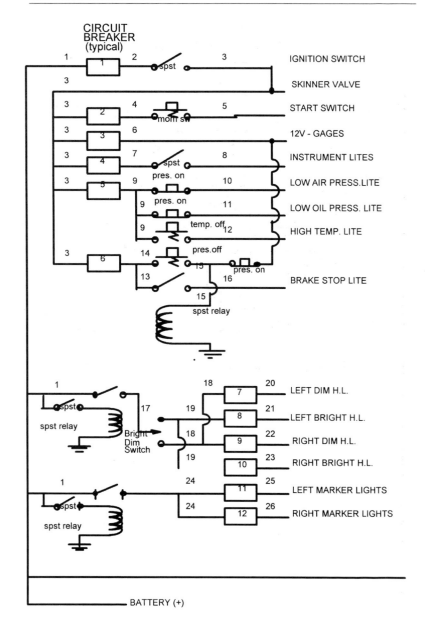

Electrical Circuits

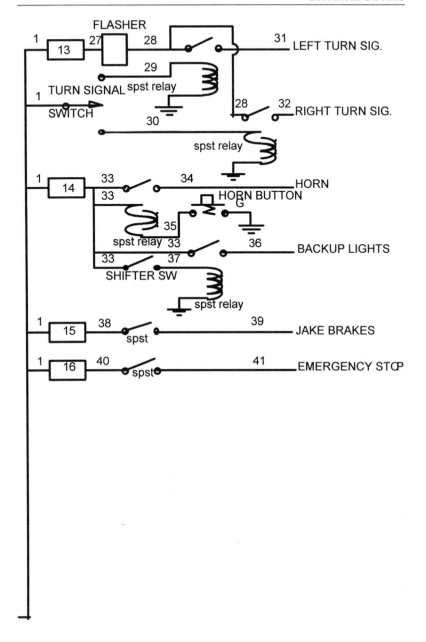

Notes:

Sketches

Chapter Twenty Six

Electronic Systems and Circuits

Modern day electronic systems for conversions include televisions, satellite receivers and coach to coach communications such as Citizen Bands radios. Other electronic systems may include central appliance control, similar to the latching relay circuits discussed in the last chapter.

Citizen band radios are rated at only two watts of transmitting power and have a normal range of only a few miles. Illegal linear amplifiers are available to couple with these radios which increase the range immensely, but are not only a violation of FCC regulations, but when too close to the target, create a distorted signal which is indecipherable. The range of the CB radio has been known to be over one thousand miles when the signal is skipped off the ionosphere. This appears to be a phenomenon of sun spots. Ham radio operators often use the phrase, *when the skip is in* and this has been shown to occur coincident with the sun spot cycles.

The performance of CB radios appear to be very erratic, but since the manufacturers are all intelligent people who know how to design and manufacture a product, you may rely on the erratic performance of CB radio being related to the antenna. A CB antenna must be tuned to the frequency being transmitted. Since the frequencies used are over a range of frequencies or a band width, as a matter of practice, CB antennas are tuned to the frequency of the middle of the band. This happens to be channel 20 in a 40-channel system. If you were going to transmit and receive only on one channel, such as channel 10, this would be the frequency to which you would tune the antenna. For this reason, you will find all the truckers on the road use channels 19 and 21, and occasionally channel 17 since they tune their antenna to the middle of the band. Each trucking corridor has its dedicated channels, such as channel 17 through the California central valley. Generally, the truckers use channel 21 east and west, and channel 19 north and south.

The length of the lead from the antenna whip to the receiver/transmitter should be in multiples of wave lengths. The common length for this coaxial cable is 22 feet. Since the cable is shielded coaxial, it is OK to coil and tie-wrap it for a neat installation. With a properly tuned antenna and the proper length of antenna cable, a normal CB radio will perform very adequately without the need for a linear amplifier. Since the CB frequency bands are line-of-sight, in the desert or the plains, the range has been known to be from three to five miles. With three or four coaches traveling in caravan, this should be quite adequate.

Television electronics include at least three sources of signal to the set. These are cable, antenna (either standard or satellite) and video tape player. Assuming you may wish to install at least two television sets, one in the living area and one in the bed room, you will need at least one switching splitter and one normal splitter. Another option may be a TV set in a baggage compartment bedroom built for your children or grandchildren. The circuitry is quite simple. From each signal source, a coaxial cable is routed to the switching splitter, and from there to the splitter sending the signal to the separate sets. The complexity goes up if two different TV sets are seeking a different signal source. In this case, a duplicate or triplicate set of circuits must be installed. The diagrams shown is a simple approach to the television circuitry described. Note one diagram is shown for a video *player*, and the other one shows a video *recorder*.

Electronic Systems and Circuits

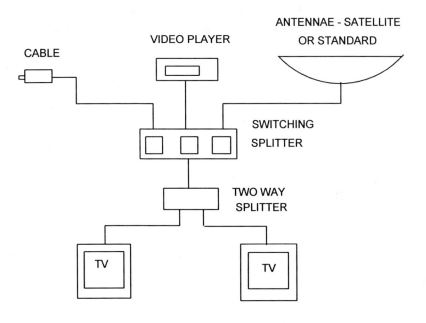

Compact disc, AM/FM radio and tape players are an essential part of living today. Plans should be made for the routing of speaker wires through out the coach, both in the upper living area and the lower section. The lower section may be used for a child's bedroom area or for simply feeding a set of patio speakers, since much of motor coach living is enjoying the outdoors under an awning.

Although, I am reticent to mention trade names in this book, Radio Shack markets a set of devices which provides a remote control system, similar to our bank of remote switches mentioned in the previous chapter. These units are made to simply plug into a wall socket and are designed to control either lamps or appliances. A master control unit is available, and is portable, or multiple master units may be placed at convenient locations. The only drawback is the bulk of the units, instead of the sanitary approach of a built-in, hard-wired, system of remote controllers.

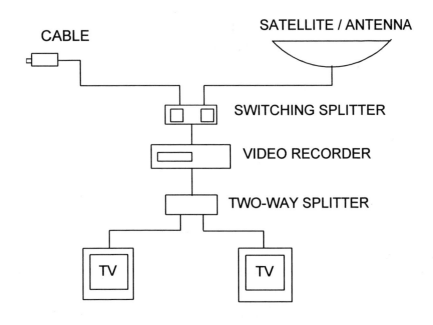

Chapter Twenty Seven

Gauges and Instrumentation

Not a lot needs to be said about the gauges on the instrument panel of the coach, with a few exceptions. Several additional gauges are useful. These are a pyrometer, a fuel pressure gauge, a tachometer, a boost pressure gauge and perhaps an altimeter. Keep in mind, gauges or meters are nothing more than devices used to indicate the current status of thing or area. Often, we may continue in ignorant bliss without the need to know these things. We certainly don't have all these gauges in our cars. Why do we need them in our coaches? Our coaches are more akin to a locomotive or an airplane than they are to a car. They are larger and more complex and less forgiving than a standard automobile. As I stated above, several additional gauges are useful, not mandatory.

The pyrometer, is a temperature gauge that indicates the exhaust gas temperature. This will help you get the best fuel economy and may be an indicator of when to change air filters. When climbing a grade, if the pyrometer can be made to show a lower temperature without the loss of speed, that is, backing your foot out of it a little, you were obviously wasting fuel. The pyrometer is really nothing more than a thermocouple of iron-constantan which generate an electrical potential (voltage), when subject to high temperatures and is calibrated to read in degrees fahrenheit.

The fuel pressure gauge is a very useful tool to determine when to change the fuel filters. It is a real dismaying experience to be traveling in a coach and sense a lessening of power and to wonder what is going wrong. With the fuel pressure gauge, the normal value will drop to about half or even less before you will feel a reduction in power from the engine. When this happens, either change the fuel filters or have it done.

A tachometer is useful in that you may see where your normal shift points are and sometimes it is wise to use your shift lever to control the engine speed for both the best performance and engine life. An altimeter is only for your own amusement. The boost pressure gauge tells you the state of your turbo-charger, and again how clean your air filter is.

Other gauges are normally standard. If you are installing, or having new gauges installed, it is recommended that they be the electrical types with senders and meters connected with wiring. Mechanical speedometers and tachometers require cable from the front of the coach to the back, and are subject to dirt and cable-windup, that is, lag. It is customary to provide temperature gauges for each bank of a V-8 motor. One oil pressure gauge is all that is necessary. The absolute minimum of instruments for a coach are: speedometer, engine oil pressure, engine water temperature, and fuel gauge.

As far as the conversion is concerned, many have no read-out meters or instruments at all. Many coaches do have, however, meters to read the house battery voltage, which is especially useful when hooking up to shore power, because it shows whether you have successfully connected power to the coach. In addition, it will show you whether the voltage is adequate. Some coaches also have an ammeter to display the amount of current being drawn.

There is an instrument developed for the marine industry known as a *BANK MANAGER*. This item of equipment reportedly will display the number of amp-hours left in your battery bank, the level of the battery voltage, and the amount of current being currently drawn. This sort of equipment would suggest to a user when it would be appropriate to turn on the generator. Another item of equipment is an automatic starter for your generator. This may be set to turn your generator on under a number of different conditions. These conditions may be, but are not limited to, a high temperature condition in the coach, or a low battery condition (see Chapter Twenty Two).

Murphy gauges are instruments that may be set with a pointer, and wired into the equipment causing it to shut down when a serious condition arises. For example, a Murphy gauge may be set at 200 degrees Fahrenheit that will cause your generator to shut down if it reaches that temperature. Earlier buses were equipped with automatic shut-downs in the event of low oil pressure, or high temperature. They were also equipped with an over-rule switch, which allowed the driver to move the coach off the highway, or maneuver it to a safe location in the event of an automatic shut-down.

Cruise controls are available that will hold speed within the range of the engine's horsepower, and are disengaged simply by stepping on the brake pedal. If the bus has an electrical speedometer sender, the cruise control is wired into the same circuit. The disengage feature is simply wired to any brake light bulb wire, so when the brake light is turned-on with your brake pedal, the cruise control disengages. Several makes of cruise controls are available. Bendix, and King are the most common.

Although remote control mirrors are not strictly gauges or instrumentation, this seems an appropriate place to mention them. The remote control mirrors are probably one of the most useful accessories which can be added to a conversion. Unless you plan to spend a lot of time traveling in very cold climates, the heated mirrors are not necessary. The combination of the wide angle and the standard mirrors, each being remotely controlled, is a super safety feature. Especially if you have to back up with low level obstructions in the vicinity of your coach. You may tilt the mirrors down in order to locate any items which may be a potential crunch point. Keep in mind, when maneuvering a vehicle as large as a bus, a simple three foot steel post does not telegraph to the driver until the bus has made contact and been damaged. A lot of damage can be done before the driver is aware there is a problem.

Finally, it is useful to have a compass to read the direction the coach is going. This can be a real problem because there is so much steel in the vicinity of the cockpit. The steel deflects the magnetic reading of the compass. Of course, there is nothing you can do about the direction you are going since you must follow the road, but sometimes it is interesting to approximate your location.

For accurate locating, the GPS (Global Positioning Satellite) receivers are now available for under three hundred dollars. They are really more useful at sea, or for off-road use, but the day is not far off the computer mapping and GPS will be affordable for highway use in a land vehicle. Some of the rental car agencies are installing them today. Currently, a system may be had for about three thousand dollars. That's a pretty expensive road map.

Part Four

Heating and Air Conditioning

The Bus converter's Bible

Chapter Twenty Eight

Basic Considerations

Determining the heating and cooling requirements for a converted coach necessitates an examination of the uses of the vehicle. The term converted coach covers a broad spectrum. Initially, the first thing comes to mind when speaking of a converted coach is a motorhome. We must, however, also consider entertainers' buses, executive coaches and special application conversions, such as, bookmobiles mobile blood banks and mobile laboratories. Each of these various types of uses demand their own heating and cooling requirements.

Motorhome conversions must be further examined for the lifestyle of the owner. For those readers who are about to specify their requirements to a custom conversion company, or plan their own, they should keep in mind the way they plan to employ their coach. Many owners simply move their coaches twice a year from one pleasant climate to another. They spend the bulk of their time in luxury parks with ample electrical power, and fully hooked up to all the amenities. Others, though they move their coach more often, still feel compelled to stay in campgrounds.

Then there are the hardy souls who prefer to blaze new trails and go where few others have gone before. These are the *Dry Campers* or also known as the *Boondockers*. They feel they have a self-contained, self-supporting vehicle, and are determined to get off the beaten path, taking full advantage of their coach. We also have the *Travelers*, the *Sight-Seer*s, the *Tourists* who believe with their coach they can travel far and wide seeing all the sights and travel in the luxury and comfort of their coach without the need to check into hotels, motels, or bed and breakfasts. This group will often park in shopping centers, state parks, private clubs, friends driveways and occasionally a campground.

It is generally agreed the heating and cooling demands of a converted motorhome should be capable of sustaining comfort under the most extremes of weather conditions. If not for the immediate owner, then for future resale value. In reviewing the various uses outlined above, the ability to be totally self-contained, and self-sustaining is paramount in the design requirements.

The entertainer coach is designed to move a group of musicians from one engagement to the next in as much comfort as possible. Generally it is a rolling dormitory, with a generous lounge area, and minimal cooking facilities. Entertainer coaches virtually never park in a campground and they seldom enjoy the use of a landline. Most often, they travel at night with the musicians sleeping, and park near the fair grounds, or concert hall after they have arrived.

The executive coach rarely contains sleeping accommodations. They are used primarily to entertain prospects, or move potential investors to sites for inspection with the prospect of sales. In addition, these coaches have been used as a means of getting department heads together, away from the normal day to day business, for brainstorming sessions. Regardless, these vehicles must be designed to provide maximum luxury and comfort for the passengers.

The special application coach conversions will probably have a more stringent design requirement. Generally, they have the public coming and going with many openings and closing of the entry door. This sort of activity causes many air changes, and the loss, or gain, of heat quite rapidly, and therefore, both the heating and the cooling requirements must be increased over a motorhome.

Basic Considerations

Although, not as severe as a public bookmobile, or a mobile blood bank, a mobile laboratory must be designed to rigid standards, especially where a controlled environment is mandatory.

In general, this section will deal with the requirements of a converted coach motorhome. The heating and cooling loads for a motorhome will be outlined using the most severe weather conditions, since we must assume at one time or another the coach will be caught in the wrong climate at the wrong time, whether it be an unseasonable heat wave in Alaska, or an uncommon freeze in Florida. Furthermore, full climate control is a sensible approach, if only from the standpoint of resale value, and the use of the coach by other individuals. This book will also recommend the necessary electrical power requirements to achieve the desired climate control. These values will be independent of any other power needs, such as lighting, cooking, entertainment, and so forth. In other words, no effort will be made in this text to determine the total power loads for a coach, only those pertaining to climate control.

Notes:

Sketches

Chapter Twenty Nine

Heating and Air Conditioning Basics

Insulation:

H eating and air conditioning loads are nothing more than a guide line to determine the performance and size of the heat producing, or heat extracting systems. The most important item to serve as the barrier to heat loss or gain is insulation.

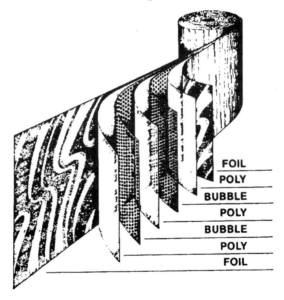

Insulation can be considered as a retardant to the flow of heat through a medium. Every material that exists has a certain level of resistance to the transfer of heat, even a material known as a conductor, such as, metal. Although any metal would be a poor choice for an insulation, each alloy does possess its resistance to heat transfer. In addition, dead air, or a dead air space has a specific resistance to heat flow. Air offers a resistance to heat flow at a rate about 15,000 times that of a good thermal conductor such as silver, and about 30 times glass. Typical insulating materials are made of nonmetallics filled with small air pockets. The insulating value decreases if the air pockets become large enough to allow thermal convection, or if moisture seeps in and acts as a conductor. Conduction and convection are ineffective in a vacuum, but radiation is very effective in a vacuum. If a reflective material is used, the heat transfer due to radiation is rejected, hence the wisdom of coating the roof of a coach with white or reflective paint.

The effectivity of the dead air space is quite evident in the use of double glazed, and sometimes triple glazed windows in residential applications. Some coach builders double glaze their fixed windows for better climate control and passenger comfort. Single layer glass not only has poor resistance to heat transfer, but in fact, tends to have an amplifying effect with heat. It will radiate heat. This is the principle reason drapes by a window are such an effective heat barrier. If sliding windows are considered in your conversion, it would be wise to employ dual pane windows if possible.

Superinsulation has recently been developed, primarily for use in space, where protection is needed against external temperatures near absolute zero. Superinsulation fabric consists of multiple sheets of aluminized mylar film, about .002 inches thick, and separated by thin spacers with about 50 to 100 layers per inch.

Many insulation materials are available and range from the very inexpensive and reasonably effective to the exotic space age superinsulation, which are quite expensive. Insulations are rated with what is known as "R" factor. "R" is the value of resistance to

Heating and Air Conditioning Basics

the flow of heat. It is also the reciprocal of the coefficient of thermal conductivity; the value of one divided by the value of R. It is not important to remember this information, only to understand the higher the R value of an insulation the more effective a heat barrier it is.

When comparing many different insulation materials, it is useful to make a cost comparison, such as is shown below.

Material	R value/inch thickness	cost per inch persq ft	Cost/R value
Rockwool	3	5 cents	1.6 cents
Urethane Foam	7	38 cents	5.4 cents
Fiberglass	3	6 cents	2.0 cents
(Superinsulation)	25	5.00[1] dollars	20.0 cents
Bubble foil	7	48 cents	6.8 cents

In normal residential applications in a cold climate, the R value of the walls are generally not less than R-11, and R- 19 to 31 for ceiling values. Since a converted coach is as close to a mobile residence as we can come, it is recommended these values be used as a target. The principle limitation in a motor coach is we do not have the wall thickness available in normal residential

---

[1] This is only a guess, since it is currently out of the range of common use, being a space age development.

construction. Although the exotic insulations are more costly, it is a prudent investment in order to achieve as much climate control as possible.

The total value of "μ", the thermal conductivity through a wall is the summation of all the values of the various materials "μ factors" plus the values of the dead air spaces, which includes the outside air film, the outside wall material, any structure, the insulation, the inside wall material, and the inside air film. The R values of the various elements are added together, and divided into one. The resultant number is the coefficient of thermal conductivity, "μ". Please make no effort to remember this information unless you are an engineer, in which case, you already know it.

Heat Loads:

The method for determining the size of the equipment to maintain comfort in any location is to calculate the amount of heat lost through the walls, the ceiling, the floor, the doors, and the windows. It is a process of computing the areas of the various elements along with their respective resistance to heat transfer using the difference in temperature in degrees to yield an answer. This answer is typically in units known as Btus, or British Thermal Units. Virtually all equipment sold in the United States is rated in Btus.

The definition of a Btu is the amount of heat required to raise one pound of water one degree Fahrenheit in one hour. The calorie, familiar to all dieters, is the metric equivalent to the Btu, except it is the amount of heat required to raise one gram of water, one degree centigrade, (Celsius) in one hour. We will not be concerned with calories in this discussion since the English speaking world uses Btus for heating and air conditioning calculations.

The human body generates approximately 100 Btus per hour when at rest. This is why a large auditorium filled with people often becomes quite stuffy as the performance progresses, especially if it is not air conditioned. A similar condition can exist in an entertainers coach in which a large number of bodies are confined in a small space. In addition, this condition mandates a minimum number of air changes per hour for comfort, normally between three and four.

A typical approach to calculating the heat loads for a coach is to determine the area, in square feet, of all the inside surfaces, that is the walls, the ceiling, and the floor. Decide the worst case outside temperature, such as minus 20 degrees Fahrenheit. Select the inside temperature you would like it to be, for example, 72 degrees. Then we take the sum of the R values, and using the reciprocal, which is the coefficient of thermal conductivity, (μ), and multiply this number times the difference in degrees, (90), and the area in square feet, and the answer we get is the number of Btus of heat loss at this extreme temperature.

As an example: 2 x length x height + 2 x length x width + 2 x width x height = gross surface area, or $A = 2(lh = lw+wh)$: l=40, h=7, w=8, ∴ **Area** = 2(40 x 7 + 40 x 8 + 8 x 7) = **1312 sq.ft.**

Temperature difference = **92 degrees**, (outside = -20, inside = 72° F.)

Assume an average **R = 11**, ∴μ = **.091, Btu heat loss** = 1312 x 92 x .091 =**10,984 Btu/hour**

Window Area = 2(2.5 x 16 +2.5 x 4.5) + 3 x 8 =126.5 μ(glass) = **1.13, Btu heat loss** (windows) = 126.5 x 92 x 1.13 = **13,151 Btu/hour**

Heat loss due to leakage = 15 percent of total = (10,745 + 13,092) x .1 = **3620 Btu/Hour**

Total Heat Loss = 10,984 + 13,151 + 3620 = **27,755 Btu/Hour**

In sizing the equipment for this example, we would use a substantial degree of conservatism, and select a heating device with at least an output of 36,000 Btu/hour, or a series of units totaling this value. This is a simplistic description of the process and the reader is not expected to remember, or even follow this approach. In fact, one of the more complex processes is to determine the total coefficient of thermal conductivity, or transmissibility through a wall made up of various elements. It is

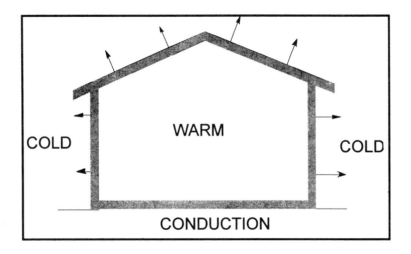

provided here only as background. Typically, the average coach will experience a 25,000 Btu to 35,000 Btu heat loss in a outside temperature of zero degrees to maintain an inside temperature of 70 degrees, depending on the quality and effectivity of the insulation, its air tightness, windows, etc.

Forms of Heat:

Heat is energy in transit; it always flows from a substance

at a higher temperature to a substance of lower temperature, thereby raising the temperature of the latter and lowering the temperature of the former, assuming the volumes do not change. Heat transfer, in physics, is a process by which energy in the form of heat is exchanged between bodies and parts of the same body at different temperatures. Heat is generally transferred by convection, radiation, or conduction. Although these three processes can occur simultaneously, it is not unusual for one mechanism to overshadow the other two. Heat, for example, is transferred by conduction through the brick wall of a house, the surfaces of high-speed aircraft are heated by convection, and the earth receives heat from the sun by radiation.

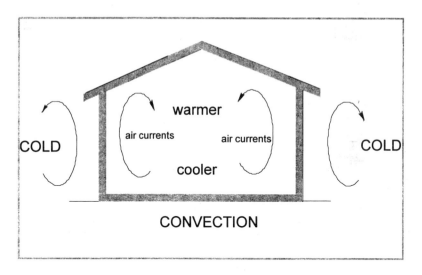

Conduction is the only method of heat transfer in opaque solids. If the temperature at one end of a metal rod is raised by heating, heat is conducted to the colder end, but the exact mechanism of heat conduction in solids is not entirely understood. It is believed, however, to be partially due to the motion of free electrons in the solid matter, which transport energy if a temperature difference is applied. This theory helps to explain why good electrical conductors also tend to be good heat conductors. Materials such as gold, silver, and copper have high thermal conductivities and conduct heat readily, but materials such as glass and asbestos have values of thermal conductivity hundreds and

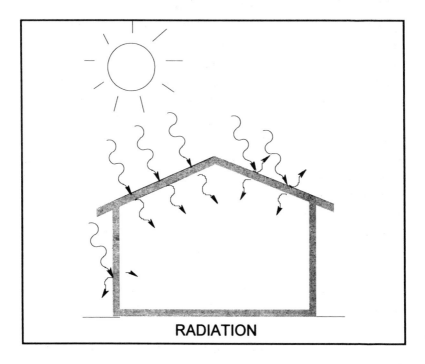

RADIATION

thousands of times smaller, conduct heat poorly, and are referred to as insulators.

Conduction occurs not only within a body but also between two bodies if they are brought into contact, and if one of the substances is a liquid or a gas, then fluid motion will almost certainly occur. This process of conduction between a solid surface

Heating and Air Conditioning Basics

and a moving liquid or gas is termed convection. The motion of the fluid may be natural or forced. If a liquid or gas is heated, its mass per unit volume generally decreases. If the liquid or gas is in a gravitational field, the hotter, lighter fluid rises while the colder, heavier fluid sinks. This kind of motion, due solely to non-uniformity of fluid temperature in the presence of a gravitational field, is called natural convection. Forced convection is achieved by subjecting the fluid to a pressure gradient and thereby forcing motion to occur according to the law of fluid mechanics. If, for example, water in a pan is heated from below, the liquid closest to the bottom expands and its density decreases; the hot water as a result rises to the top and some of the cooler fluid descends toward the bottom, thus setting up a circulatory motion. Similarly, in a vertical gas-filled chamber, such as the air space between two window panes in a double-glazed, or *Thermopane*, window, the air near the cold outer pane will move down and the air near the inner, warmer pane will rise, leading to a circulatory motion. The heating of a room by a radiator depends less on radiation than on natural convection currents, the hot air rising upward along the wall and cooler air falling back to the radiator. Because of the tendencies of hot air to rise and of cool air to sink, for maximum efficiency, radiators should be placed near the floor, and air-conditioning outlets near the ceiling. Natural convection is also responsible for the rising of the hot water and steam in natural convection boilers and for the draft in a chimney. Convection also determines the movement of large air masses above the earth, such as the action of the winds, rainfall, ocean currents, and the transfer of heat from the interior of the sun to its surface.

Radiation, as a process, is fundamentally different from both conduction and convection; the substances exchanging heat need not be in contact with each other. They can, in fact, be separated by a vacuum. Radiation is a term generally applied to all kinds of electromagnetic wave phenomena. Opaque surfaces can absorb or reflect incident radiation. Generally dull, rough surfaces absorb more heat than bright, polished surfaces and bright surfaces reflect more radiant energy than dull surfaces. In addition, good absorbers are also good emitters; good reflectors, or poor absorbers, are poor emitters. Thus, cooking utensils generally have dull bottoms for good absorption and polished sides for minimum emission to maximize the net heat transfer into the contents of the pot. Some substances, such as gases and glass, are capable of transmitting large amounts of radiation. It is experimentally observed the absorbing, reflecting, and transmitting properties of a substance depend upon the wavelength of the incident radiation. Glass, for example, transmits large amounts of short wavelength (ultraviolet) radiation, and is a poor transmitter of long wavelength (infrared) radiation.

The greenhouse effect is where the radiant energy from the sun is transmitted through the glass and enters the greenhouse. The energy emitted by the contents of the greenhouse which emit primarily at infrared wavelengths, is not transmitted out through the glass. Thus, although the air temperature outside the greenhouse may be low, the temperature inside the greenhouse will be much higher because there is a sizable net heat transfer into it.

In addition to heat transfer processes which result in raising or lowering temperatures of the participating bodies, heat transfer can also produce phase changes such as the melting of ice or the boiling of water. In engineering, heat transfer processes are usually designed to take advantage of these phenomena. In the case of space capsules re-entering the atmosphere of the earth at very high speed a heat shield which melts in a prescribed manner by a process called ablation occurs to prevent overheating of the interior of the capsule. Essentially, the frictional heating produced by the atmosphere is used to melt the heat shield and not

Heating and Air Conditioning Basics

to raise the temperature of the capsule.

Energy Sources:

All heating and cooling devices require energy in some form to operate. Perhaps the most useful fuel is the common fuel for the motor, diesel fuel. However, one primary consideration in this respect is, although it would be more convenient to draw from a single tank, fuel for heating is not taxed as road fuel. Therefore, it would be wise to consider adding a separate tank dedicated to heating fuel. In addition, in an emergency under either condition, fuel from one could be used for the other application. Stringent regulation are in effect when it comes to using home heating fuel for your vehicle engine. I recently heard of one penalty, which was to fine the offender at the rate of one hundred dollars per gallon of off road fuel found in their primary engine tank. Off road fuel is dyed red and as such it is unmistakable.

In the less expensive conversions, propane is the fuel of choice. Many heating devices are manufactured to employ propane. Caution must be used when installing a propane system. It is a very volatile gas, and is heavier than air. This feature makes propane especially hazardous in marine applications where it is impossible to allow the gas to drain overboard. Sniffers and exhaust fans are routinely employed in marine installations to prevent accidents.

Customarily, the propane tanks are installed in the baggage compartments, and are vented in the floor so any leakage will drain out and not build up. Furthermore, the area where the propane tanks are installed should be compartmented with full bulkheads, so no leakage can migrate to other areas, where perhaps a water heater might reside (see Chapter 19). Propane fuel is very economical, and will last for a long period. Many manufactured motorhomes use propane with permanently mounted tanks. This design requires the vehicle be driven to the propane station for refueling, whereas, if portable tanks were employed, they could be disconnected from the coach and taken to the refueling depot in a tow car without having to move the coach. When designing your conversion, this is a convenience which should be considered.

Without question, electricity is the safest form of energy for heating. When parked in a campground or RV park, electrical power is readily available. However, some campgrounds do not have

the capacity to provide adequate electrical power for the *all electric coaches*. Even modern day luxury parks with their 50 ampere service will be hard pressed to deliver enough power to drive three air conditioning units, coupled with a water heater cycling, and electric cooking simultaneously. In many of the more luxurious conversions, generators capable of delivering 150 amperes are not uncommon.

Keep in mind when considering electrically generated heat, the required energy must be created from a fuel source when away from the land-line, or shore power. Again, all form of fuel are used to generate this electricity, so in a way electrical power is simply another step in energy conversion. Electrical generators may be driven with all the fuels noted above, plus gasoline. Obviously, it would be much more convenient to use a diesel driven generator, hence the discussion regarding off-road fuel above.

Solar power has been developed in two discreet forms. The photovoltaic cell converts sunlight directly into electrical energy. We are all familiar with the light emitting diode (LED), which when impressed with a voltage, lights up. The photovoltaic cell, or solar panel is the inverse of the LED, whereby when light impinges upon it a voltage is generated. Solar panels came on the scene about forty years ago, and cost about three dollars a watt. As with all electronic breakthroughs, it was expected the cost would reduce dramatically. However, in this application it was not to be. Today, solar panels generally cost about four to five dollars per watt, making them unusually expensive. Since the heating requirements of a coach may be on the order of 5 to 10 kilowatts, the roof of the vehicle could not contain enough solar panels to be effective. The photovoltaic solar panel is quite effective as a passive battery charger, but that is another subject.

Although, it is not recommended for a coach conversion, the other form of solar energy should be mentioned. During each sunlight hour of the day, approximately 280 Btus of solar energy fall upon each square foot of the earth. Of course, the actual figure varies with the time of day, the clarity of the air, the time of the year and the latitude. In a well designed building, this energy can be more than enough to provide all the comfort necessary. Supplemental heating methods must be employed to carry through periods of inclement weather and periods of darkness. The common method is to use roof panels with built-in water circuits. The water then flows into tanks, or reservoirs, which becomes a source for the heat. This is especially useful when a heat pump is employed. Even though this concept has some degree of feasibility, the aesthetics of the coach would be severely compromised, along with the added space needed to store a reservoir and the heat pump system.

Safety:

     Safety in a heating system is not only the intrinsic safety, but the perceived safety. Many people thoughout the country are afraid of natural gas for heating and cooking. In the Southwest where the public grew up with this form of energy, it is an accepted way of life. Others in the Northeast are more accustomed to heating oil and feel comfortable with it.

     Heating with electricity, if properly designed, may be the safest form of heat although diesel fired boilers with circulating pumps can be considered very safe. Diesel fuel is an energy source with a high degree of Btus per pound, and is inherently safe; it takes a fair degree of energy just to ignite diesel oil. Back in the days when almost everyone smoked it was common in the engine rooms of navy and coast guard ships to have a coffee can of diesel fuel sitting in front of the boiler just to pitch our cigarette butts in. The lit cigarette butts would simply be extinguished in the raw diesel fuel.

Heating and Air Conditioning Basics

One of the principal advantages of either heating with electricity, or diesel is there will be no products of combustion inside the living area. This feature, of course, is designed into the RV style propane heaters, with both the combustion air and products of combustion being transported to and from outside the coach. This feature renders this type of heater quite inefficient, since much of the heat is pumped overboard. Many wall type heaters, such as the catalytic heater, unless positively vented will consume much of the interior oxygen, thus creating an unsafe atmosphere. All catalytic heaters, unless positively vented, have an admonition to be used with plenty of ventilation.

Ventilation:

Buildings in which people live and work must be ventilated to replenish oxygen, dilute the concentration of carbon dioxide and water vapor, and minimize unpleasant odors. A certain amount of air movement or ventilation ordinarily is provided by air leakage through small crevices in the building's walls, especially around windows and doors. Such haphazard ventilation may suffice for homes, but not for public buildings such as offices, theaters, and factories, or in fact, coaches with their tight fitting windows and doors.

Engineers estimate for adequate ventilation the air in a room should be changed completely from one and a half to three times each hour. 280 to 850 liters (about 10 to 30 cu ft) of fresh air-per-minute should be supplied for each occupant. Providing this amount of ventilation usually requires mechanical devices to augment the natural flow of air. Simple ventilation devices include fans or blowers arranged either to exhaust the stale air from the building or to force fresh air into the building, or both. Ventilating systems may be combined with heaters, filters, humidity controls, or cooling devices. Many systems include heat exchangers. These use outgoing air to heat or cool incoming air, thereby increasing the efficiency of the system by reducing the amount of energy needed to operate it.

Many motorcoaches have fixed windows so the occupants have no option but to be content with the air changes or ventilation designed into the bus by the manufacturers. When considering a coach conversion, if the bus has fixed windows, the prospective owner should consider changing the windows so as to provide sliders, or other ways of opening the windows to allow fresh air to circulate. Custom windows are now available for virtually all makes of buses. These may be installed at the option of the owner. Or special windows may be installed by a conversion company to meet the owners needs.

Air filters are available in at least two styles. First is the simple air filter common in all residential applications, which is nothing more than a matted matrix of fibers which filter out they heaviest particulate. Then, there is the electrostatic filter system which will filter the smallest pollen and has been available for residential installation for about 25 years. For those who suffer from airborne allergies, the electrostatic filter would alleviate considerable suffering. This system must be installed in a central heating and air conditioning source, since to be effective, it requires virtually all the air circulating within the coach, pass through it.

Chapter Thirty

Heating

Original Equipment, Factory Installed

Every bus leaves the factory with a carefully engineered heating and air conditioning system. This equipment is designed and sized to provide comfort for up to nearly 50 passengers. This is especially significant with respect to cooling loads, when you consider each passenger is capable of generating approximately 100 Btus/hour, or an additional heating load of 5,000 Btus/ hour.

For traveling comfort in a converted coach it is strongly recommended this system be left intact. The air conditioning system in a bus is a high maintenance item, but to duplicate this system with other methods is like re-inventing the wheel. Why bother? Arguments are offered this system is useless when parked, or when camping. Although this is true and obviously supplemental climate control must be added, a conversion company will be hard pressed to duplicate, and/or improve on the factory installed climate control system. The principal disadvantage to the factory installed heating and cooling system is it occupies approximately 50 to 60 cubic feet which might be used for other applications. As an example, many older Eagle coach conversions use the space previously occupied by the air conditioning condenser to install a diesel driven generator. In addition, the space previously used to house the evaporator and blowers may be used to house extra fuel storage.

Perhaps in the older coaches, removal of the factory installed equipment may be justified, but in buses less than ten years old, the equipment is just not that obsolete. The prospective owner would do well to consider retaining this equipment, not only for his comfort, but for future resale value.

Assuming you have decided to retain the original heating and cooling system, it is obvious that this system is not useful when you are parked. What should you add for heating comfort while parked in a campground, a state park, or near a quiet stream? A myriad of answers come to mind. Let's examine each one.

Diesel Boiler

The first system which comes to mind is the diesel fired boiler. The heart of this system is a package about the size of two footballs, end to end. It uses engine radiator coolant pumped past a diesel burner, then circulated throughout the coach to individual radiators, or radiant finned units with individual fans similar to baseboard heaters, to extract the heat and deliver it to each compartment. The coolant is then re-circulated to the burner section to repeat the action. One system uses a single loop, so by the time it is nearing the end of its loop, most of the heat has already been extracted. A more efficient system uses two loops. One loop circulates only hot water while the other loop returns cooler water whose heat has been extracted. Make-up water to the burner is drawn from a reservoir, while the return cool water is delivered to the reservoir. This system is thermostatically controlled, which automatically ignites the burner, activates the circulating pump, and turns on the fans at the individual radiator units. One major advantage to this system is it also serves as an engine preheater, since engine coolant may be circulated through a heat exchanger. This can be a very useful thing in cold weather. Diesel engines can be very stubborn to start when cold.

Heating

Several brands of this type of heating system are available. Probably the most well known brand of this type heating system is the Webasto. The Webasto system comprises the boiler heating a coolant in a closed loop, supplying heat to various fan/heater elements back through an expansion tank to be recirculated. Although copper piping with its soldered joints is an ideal material for circulating the coolant, the risk of fire from the installation and soldering of the pipe and its fittings has caused other materials to be used. An excellent substitute for the copper piping is ¾-inch diameter heater hose.the hose may be swept in gradual turns, and where an abrupt bend is needed, a copper fitting prepared outside the coach may be coupled with the hose. The spring loaded type hose clamps are recommended since they apply a

constant pressure regardless of the temperature. There are also various high temperature plastic piping systems now available which will function in a satisfactory manner. The maximum temperature routed through the heating system is 180 degrees Fahrenheit.

    The coolant for the heating system must be a mixture of 50/50 — water and antifreeze. This circuit will be totally independent from the coach engine cooling, but through a heat exchanger may be used to preheat the motor. The circuit is normally a parallel circuit sending hot water out to the various fan/heater units and returning cooler water to the boiler through and expansion tank. It is essential the expansion tank be above the level of the boiler, and accessible. This tank is often placed inside a closet. In this circuit it is mandatory there be no air entrapment. In the event small bubbles are encountered, the boiler may cause a high temperature safety fuse to burn out and the unit will not function until it has been replaced. It is for this reason the water circuit be isolated from the engine coolant, in that tiny bubbles can develop in the engine water that are eventually eliminated through the radiator cap. The flow rate of the coolant is normally about 6 gallons per minute so that ¾-inch hose provides adequate flow rate over about 100 feet of circuitry and three full flow fan/heater units.

    Heat exchangers are available for not only preheating the engine, but for providing domestic hot water for bathing and cooking. In addition, electric water heaters are available with built in heat exchangers so hot water may be obtained from shore power, generator power, or from the Webasto boiler unit. Circuitry has been developed so in summer months when no heat is needed, the boiler will supply hot water to the heat exchanger for domestic hot

Heating

water.

 Diesel fuel to the boiler unit should have its own supply line rather than teeing-off of the main fuel line to the engine. A tee intersecting the main engine supply fuel line has been tried in the past and has consistently caused problems. The fuel supply to the boiler unit is similar to the engine in that it has a supply and a return. A specific tank should be dedicated to the heating unit for reasons mentioned earlier in this book; the lesser cost off-road fuel may be used for heating. This tank should supply both the heating system and the generator.

 The unit should be mounted in such a manner it may be accessible for maintenance and it would be a good idea to provide soundproofing around the containment box. Both the boiler and the circulating pump can be noisy. A further contributor to the high noise level is the exhaust pipe, which must be routed outside.

 Individual fan/heaters are available to be placed in strategic locations. These units, on average, produce about 7,000 Btus each. The entire system may be controlled by thermostats, or a combination of thermostats. For example, three units may be controlled by a thermostat in the living room/kitchen area, and another two units may be controlled by a thermostat in the bathroom, or bedroom area. Another more passive heater is available in the form of a baseboard finned unit. The baseboard finned units can be had in the form of 2 x 2 inch fins along a ¾-inch pipe in almost any length. These non fan baseboard heaters are customarily set about 1½ inches above the floor or carpet along the baseboard. The cold dense air slides down the wall from the windows, is heated by convection and rises to replace the cold air. Another fan/heater unit from Webasto is the toe-kick size which may be installed under the cabinet in the recessed kick area such as a bathroom cabinet or the kitchen counter. Each of the fan/heater units have either an in-line or elbow air bleed fitting on the downstream side to make sure no air resides in the circuitry.

The Webasto coolant heaters can be ordered in 12VDC and 24VDC configurations and have heating capacities ranging from 16,000 Btus to 160,000 Btus. Perhaps the most useful size for a conversion is the Model DWB2010 whose output is 40,000 Btus. Webasto also markets an air heater with capacities ranging from 6,000 Btus to 40,000 Btus. I am currently unaware of any converted coach employing the use of the Webasto air heaters. The average electrical power consumption is about 5½ amperes at 12VDC, and about ⅔ of a gallon of diesel fuel per hour.

A competitor to the Webasto is a newer product with the trade name PROHEAT, manufactured by Teleflex. This unit was originally developed as an engine pre-heater for large diesel trucks operating in very cold areas of North America. ProHeat produces two sizes, a 30,000 Btu and a 50,000 Btu unit. Since the ProHeat device is a much newer product than the Webasto, it employs newer technology. It has a computerized controller with memory which may be down loaded into a personal computer. This allows the system to be diagnosed by a service station to determine the last 50 starts, to see if, for example, a low voltage was present. Other readouts include number of hours, water temperature, number of cycles and other parameters. It also uses a compressor to finely atomize the combustion air to the fuel nozzle for more efficient burning.

The big market for the ProHeat is the trucking industry, not converted coach sales. Hence, service stations are being located all over the country. These units are being installed on new trucks for several reasons. The newer engines such as the Detroit Series

60 do not produce sufficient heat for heating the cab, so auxiliary heaters must be employed. In addition, due to the Clean Air Act, in many location trucks are not permitted to idle, so again, auxiliary heaters must be used. Many of the newer production coaches are including diesel fired boilers for passenger heat and defrosting.

The ProHeat system is comparable to the Webasto in performance and cost. The principal difference is the ProHeat is a newer design using the latest technology. And because of the truck market, more service stations are available. A rough order of magnitude cost for a complete ProHeat system is about $3,300. This figure includes four space heaters, thermostats, valves, expansion tank, a heat exchanger for engine heat, and a heat exchanger domestic water heater. Again, this represents the components less the piping and installation labor.

The AquaHot system uses the Webasto heater, but is effectively an engineered system with all controls and plumbing, and is probably the top of the line when it comes to diesel heating for motor coaches.

Electric Heaters:

Electric heating generally costs more than energy obtained from the combustion of a fuel, but the convenience, cleanliness, and reduced space needs of electric heat can often justify its use. The heat can be provided from electric coils or strips used in varying patterns. For example, convectors may be in or on the walls, under windows, or as baseboard radiation. Electric heating is one of the safer forms of heat. In addition to being safe, the electric heater also is convenient to install, and might be located in areas which are unused. Since heated air tends to be displaced by colder more dense air, consequently rising, the obvious location for a heater, regardless of their energy source, is near the floor.

One form of an electric heater is a small thermostatically controlled unit mounted in the toe-kick area underneath cabinets and furniture (see the photograph below). The unit is appropriately

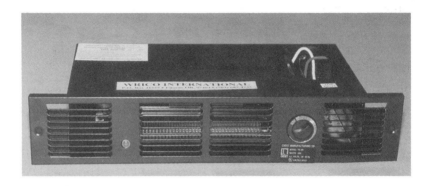

WRICO INTERNATIONAL

call the Perfect-Toe. This unit is 3½ inches high, and 17 inches wide, by 10 inches deep. It is capable of producing 1000 watts of heat, and has a built-in thermostat switch. To compare this output with our heat load in Btus, each kilowatt-hour of electricity equals 3412 Btus. Each one of these toe-kick heaters generate 3412 Btus. In my personal coach I use four of these units, augmented with two 6000 Btu Catalytic heaters, and have been comfortable in sub-zero weather in Utah. The only drawback to this unit is that each unit has its own controls, so that they are not centrally controlled. However, a simple circuit could be designed that would

Heating

control all the units in a coach from a single thermostat, after each unit had been tuned to its optimum performance.

Another form of electric heat is the baseboard heater. One drawback to this design is that much of the baseboard around a coach is occupied by built-in furniture, or other permanently mounted facilities. Still, it would be a simple matter to route the heating elements in such as way to become part of the built in furniture, or other facilities.

Propane Heaters

In most motorhomes and lower cost conversions, propane is the fuel of choice. Propane is an odorless gas, and is one of the fractions of crude oil. An agent is added to propane which gives it a distinctive odor of strong garlic. A propane leak is very easy to detect with its distinctive smell.

The Primus system is similar to the Webasto except for the fuel, which is propane. The Primus boiler is shown to the left. The Primus system has similar types of heaters as Webasto, but they stress the passive radiant fin baseboard type. It may be considered the top of the line for propane.

The RV industry has developed many options for propane heaters. The most common propane heater is the forced air type, which takes in outside air to support combustion, exhausts theproducts of combustion to the outside, and heats a rad iator section over which air is blown. This heated air may be blown directly into the living compartment, or directed through a series of 4-inch
 ducts to strategic locations. The outlet of these ducts may be controlled with a register which may be throttled with dampers, or movable vanes used to attenuate the flow of air. The most significant drawback to this type of heater is its poor efficiency

rating. Since, for safety, it must draw in outside air for combustion and expel these products of combustion, much of the heat is pumped overboard. This is patently obvious if you have ever stood next to one of these exhaust ports in the winter and felt the heat being expelled. Regardless of this inefficiency, propane as a heating fuel is relatively inexpensive, and these heaters can do an effective job of heating a coach. Such units are normally installed in a closet, or inside a table, or beneath a bench seat, or even in the baggage compartment, so one side is adjacent to an outside wall. Most are thermostatically controlled and are operated by a 12VDC current.

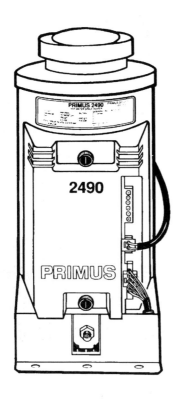

Several brands names are available for this type of furnace. They are: Suburban, by Dometic, and Hydra-Flame, by Hydra-Flame.

Catalytic Heaters

Another, more effective form of propane heater is the catalytic heater. This heater uses a platinum mesh and fiber matrix which allows the fuel to burn without a flame. The burning in this matrix will glow and produces a radiate form of heat. It is actually a form of convection combined with radiation, with the prominent

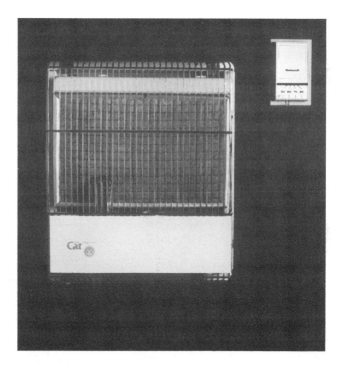

form being radiation. These units are mounted as a wall unit, which is a draw back since wall space in a conversion is a premium..

The less sophisticated units use a mechanical pizzo-electric igniter, similar to those seen on barbecues. While striking the igniter, a gas valve must be held down to light the pilot. After the pilot is lit, the main gas valve may be opened as desired. This unit requires no electric power to the installation, only a source of propane. The Olympia catalytic heater is an example of this kind.

The Platinum Cat, produced by Thermal Systems of Washington, is a well engineered catalytic heater which uses a tiny blower to vent products of combustion through a small duct to the outside, and is thermostatically controlled with an automatic igniter. The unit must be supplied with a 12VDC power source, along with a supply of propane. Again, the unit must be mounted on a vertical surface similar to the old fashioned wall heaters installed in the cheapest houses built after World War II. I have seen this unit installed in an area over the drivers section located behind cabinet doors. This form of installation is not recommended, but with adequate heat shields on the inside of the cabinets, and doors, and with a fail-safe interlock so the unit is disabled when the doors are closed, this installation appears to be satisfactory.

Although the following two paragraphs have appeared elsewhere in this book (Chapter 19), it bears repeating for the sake of emphasis. Propane requires another fuel be carried along in the conversion. It is customary in many production motorhomes to install a permanently mounted tank to store propane. This type of installation requires the coach be driven to the propane filling station for re-fueling. At times this can be inconvenient, and especially when the maneuvering room is limited. A more convenient installation is to use portable tanks which may be disconnected from the coach and taken to the re-fueling location in a car, or other smaller vehicle. Propane is stored as a liquid at high pressure and reduces to a gas at very low pressures. A pressure

Heating

regulator is installed between the storage tanks and the service line. Black iron pipe is the material of choice for propane distribution throughout the coach. The one-half inch iron piping is routed close to the appliance, then a gas cock is installed. Chapter Nineteen shows schematic options. From the gas cock, which allows the appliance to be disconnected from service, a propane hose is routed to the appliance, using 45 degree flare fitting connectors. It is important each appliance being served by propane be able to be isolated and disconnected. Another form of installation is to feed the low pressure propane from the pressure regulator into a manifold with a series of gas cocks, one for each appliance. From that point an LPG hose may be run to each appliance. It is mandatory that only hose which is clearly marked LPG be used. This sort of hose has the approval of the Underwriters Laboratories. If another material is used and there is an accident, the insurance claim would certainly be denied. It is commonly believed copper piping would be acceptable for propane distribution. Copper is outlawed in California for LPG because the odor causing agent added to commercial propane is highly corrosive to copper alloys.

    Diesel and propane heating systems require a specific minimal electric power to operate The equipment requiring the most electrical power would be the diesel fired boiler, which uses power to drive the circulating pump and the individual fans or blowers at each radiator. Next would be the forced air heater, which needs power to ignite the unit and operate the blowers to circulate the forced air. Finally, the lowest power drain would be the catalytic heater with its tiny ventilation blower and automatic igniter

Normally, the concept of heating the baggage compartments would not be considered. This may be worth an examination in the event water pipes are routed through this space. Some form of

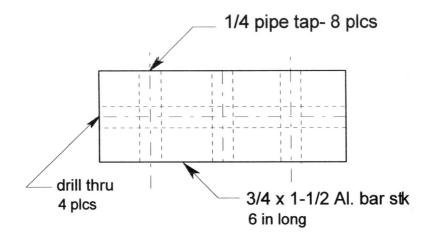

Propane Distribution Manifold

thermostatically controlled heat would be very prudent in any space occupied by water piping if the colder climates are visited. Although, hot and cold water pipes are available that are freeze resistant, there is a temperature below which virtually no pipe can stand up. Even if the water piping is made of heater hose, which will not break if it freezes, the inconvenience of frozen pipes is worth the effort to keep them ice free. A simple way of heating pipes is to wrap with a tape made just for this purpose. A built in thermostat will turn on the heat tape at about 35 degrees.

Heat Pumps

For background purposes a brief discussion of heat pumps is included. A heat pump is a system designed to provide useful heating and cooling, and its actions are essentially the same for either process. Instead of creating heat, as does a furnace, the heat pump transfers heat from one place to another. In cold weather, a liquid refrigerant such as Freon, is pumped through a coil which is outside the area to be heated. The refrigerant is cold, so it absorbs heat from the outside air, the ground, well water, or some other source. It then flows first to a compressor, which raises its temperature and pressure so it becomes vapor before it flows to an indoor coil. There the warmth is radiated or blown into the room or other space to be heated. The refrigerant, having given up much of its heat, then flows through a valve where its pressure and temperature are lowered further before it liquefies and is pumped into the outdoor coil to continue the cycle.

To air condition a space, valves reverse the flow so the refrigerant picks up heat from inside and discharges it outside. Like furnaces, most heat pumps are controlled by thermostats. Most heat pumps use atmospheric air as their heat source. This presents a problem in areas where winter temperatures frequently drop below freezing, making it difficult to raise the temperature and pressure of the refrigerant. Heat-pump systems are now being used extensively not only in residences but also in commercial buildings and schools.

For further information regarding heat pumps for recreational vehicles, see **Chapter Thirty Two**, page 210.

Notes:

Sketches

Chapter Thirty One

Ventilation

As mentioned previously in this book, ventilation is an essential design requirement for any heating and cooling installation. Simply to maintain a comfortable climate, the air in a coach should be changed at least two to three times per hour. This requirement increases as the inside activity, or as the number of people occupying the coach increases. On average the ventilating system should be capable of expelling approximately 6,000 cubic feet per hour, or about 100 cfm (cubic feet per minute).

Two methods of air changes are available; passive and active. Passive ventilation is nothing more than having windows which may be opened to allow air to enter the coach and using roof vents to allow air to exhaust. This form of ventilation may be enhanced by using roof vents with built in fans. Several products of this nature are available. AlumaKool and Coolamatic are brands which use a slow moving wide blade fan that act quite similar to an attic fan in a house. These might be considered the least expensive products. Their principal advantage is they move a great deal of air with a whisper quiet noise factor. Their principal disadvantage is they are somewhat unsightly from the outside because they protrude above the roof similar to a roof air conditioner. In addition, they must be manually turned on and off.

Fantastic Vents brand name is next in line and offers several models. The Fantastic Vent uses a smaller, higher speed fan which has three speeds. Using this design allows them to create a much smaller, more attractive package. Their external appearance shows no more profile than a standard RV ventilation dome. They also offer a thermostatically controlled unit which will automatically open the vent, and then turn on the fan, and close the vent and shut down the fan. Furthermore, they have a unit which will sense rain, and automatically close the vent, and stop the fan. They also offer a combination of all the various features listed. The principal disadvantage to this product, when compared to the attic fan style mentioned earlier, is the noise factor can be somewhat irritating, even when set at their slowest speed.

Another form of passive ventilation is to install a moonroof or a sunroof. The moonroof, is distinguished from the sunroof by having a sliding hatch which blocks out the light. These units are available from several sources as after-market accessories for the automotive trade. One additional advantage to this sort of unit is it may serve a dual purpose. It may become an escape hatch or even an entry hatch to the roof. It is not uncommon to have a small patio with collapsible guard rails and a canopy installed on the roof of a custom conversion. This is especially delightful to use when attending a sporting event such as a race or other outside activity.

For people who are sensitive to airborne irritants, Honeywell has made available to the market a unit which scrubs the air in a coach approximately six times per hour. This product is known as an *Enviracaire* and is rated as a class II medical device. This means that it may be prescribed by a doctor and is tax deductible. It is portable, about the size of a small stool, and will filter airborne particulate matter down to 3 microns. To put this in perspective, an average human hair is about 12 microns thick, or to be more precise, a micron is 0.0004 inches across. This product has a rating of HEPA, meaning high efficiency particulate air. This designation has a more significant meaning for those people suffering from airborne allergies.

In very cold, or very hot weather, passive ventilation, i.e., opening windows and roof vents are not acceptable. In these applications, positive ventilation must be accomplished with the heating and cooling equipment. This is normally done with duct work routed throughout the coach providing positive air flow with return registers for recycling the heated or cooled air with make up air. This sort of design provides minimal air changes for ventilation.

Ducts may be routed through the baggage compartment, or the ceiling. Another convenient location for ducts are along the baseboard, above or below the floor line, and above the window headers and behind cabinet work. Ducts must be sized large enough to minimize the noise factor. Too high an air flow through ducts which are too small will create an irritating noise level. Registers that are too small will cause an annoying whistle sound. If your conversion specialist is not competent in this area, or you have any questions, it would be wise to consult an HVAC engineer and have any duct work sized for your comfort.

Although awnings are not normally classified as part of heating, ventilating and air conditioning equipment, they do provide improved ventilation for a coach. Specifically window

awnings may be extended which will do two things; shade the interior of the coach from unwelcome direct sunlight, and enhance the flow of fresh air through openable windows. Even if the windows are not operable, the shading of the interior from direct sunlight is a positive step.

Chapter Thirty Two

Air Conditioning

At this point I would like to repeat myself, and remind the reader that as the bus left the factory, it possessed a fully functioning, well engineered cooling system designed to provide comfort for many more passengers than the reader plans to carry. You are again admonished, "Why fight success?" Unless your coach shell is very old and the air conditioning system is antiquated, it would pay you in comfort and future resale value of your conversion to invest at least half the cost of good diesel driven generator to have your coach refrigerated air conditioning upgraded to the latest government regulations. No doubt, if you have a newer coach, plans have already been made to allow an upgrade. Eagle, Prevost, Neoplan, and MCI no doubt have something in the works as this is being written. Even if you have an older, more vintage coach with the equipment still intact, you would be well advised to seek the council of a reputable automotive air conditioning specialist, to determine what would be needed to bring your shell into compliance with DOT standards.

Keep in mind that automotive air conditioning began around fifty to sixty years ago. I remember as a child in the 1930s crossing the desert from Oklahoma to California, and sitting on a pillow with a chunk of dry ice underneath it (no, I was not a Grapes of Wrath child). This was perhaps the original automotive air. The next year, inm 1937 when we made our annual vacation trip to California, we had the latest piece of equipment available at the time; a window evaporative air conditioner. This looked like an eight or ten-inch diameter cylinder about two feet long with an opening at the leading edge, a vent into the car and a water tank. Periodically we would fill the water tank and as we drove forward (at a maximum speed of about 50), the ram air would cause a cylinder filled with excelsior (a matte of fine wood strips) to rotate through the water saturating the excelsior and cooling the hot air, thus allowing the cooled air to vent into the vehicle.

Later, of course, cars were equipped with refrigerated air conditioning systems. Even today, evaporative coolers are available and are quite effective in hot dry climates. But since the reader is considering a conversion which will be able to go anywhere, with occupant comfort in mind and have good resale value, this will be the sum and substance of our discussion of evaporative cooling.

Theory

The air conditioning we will discuss from this point forward is confined exclusively to refrigerated air. The design requirements of the air conditioning loads are similar to the discussion we had earlier with reference to calculating the number of Btus heat loss, and in this application we will be concerned with the Btu heat gain. If a wall, or other barrier has a certain resistance to the flow of heat out, it is logical to assume it has the same resistance regardless of which way the heat is flowing. So, if you are attempting to maintain a specific temperature value inside a coach when the outside value has increased, you still have a temperature differential producing a specific number of Btus heat gain. Let us assume you might wish to visit Furnace Creek at Death Valley. You plan for a February visit when the normal outside temperature is about 85 degrees, but along comes a summer day in February and the temperature rises to 140 degrees Fahrenheit.

Air Conditioning

So, what kind of air conditioning load does this create? Returning to our heat load calculations using a 70 degree temperature differential, it will be obvious our heat gain will approach between 25,000 and 30,000 Btus per hour. A number of years ago, it was fashionable to rate air conditioning units in tons of cooling. The value of a ton of air conditioning was the amount of heat needed to melt a ton of ice in 24 hours. Now it is common to use 12,000

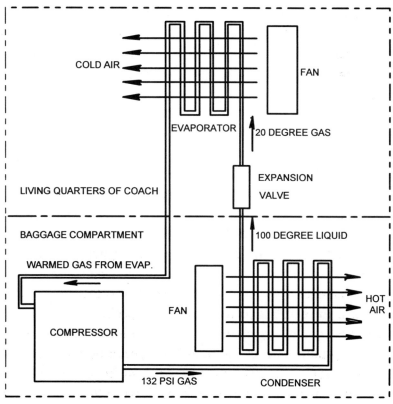

SCHEMATIC OF AIR CONDITIONING CYCLE
D.GALEY 6-16-95

Btus/hour which is equal to one ton of cooling. Horsepower ratings were formerly used for small air conditioners, but the term is misleading because a horsepower (or 746 watts) represents work power and not cooling. It came into use because under usual summer conditions a motor of one horsepower could support 3.5 kw of cooling, the equivalent of a ton of refrigeration.

A brief discussion of the way a refrigerated unit works is in order at this point. First, it must be pointed out there are two basic forms of refrigeration systems, compression system and absorption system. In mechanical refrigeration, constant cooling is achieved by the circulation of a refrigerant in a closed system, which evaporates to a gas and then condenses back again to a liquid in a continuous cycle. If no leakage occurs, the refrigerant lasts indefinitely throughout the entire life of the system. All that is required to maintain cooling is a constant supply of energy, or power, and a method of dissipating waste heat. The two main types of mechanical refrigeration systems are the compression system, used in domestic units for large cold-storage applications and for most air conditioning, and the absorption system, now employed largely for heat-operated air-conditioning units but formerly also used for heat-operated domestic units. The standard RV refrigerator uses the absorption system.

Compression Systems

Compression systems employ four elements in the refrigeration cycle: compressor, condenser, expansion valve, and evaporator. In the evaporator the refrigerant is vaporized and heat is absorbed from the material contents or the space being cooled. The vapor next is drawn into a motor-driven compressor and elevated to high pressure, which raises its temperature. The resulting

Air Conditioning

superheated, high-pressure gas is then condensed to liquid in an air- or water-cooled condenser. The heat absorbed in the evaporator phase is expelled in the condenser phase by blowing air over the condenser or washing it with water. From the condenser the liquid flows through an expansion valve, in which its pressure and temperature are reduced to the conditions maintained in the evaporator. A fan normally blows air over the evaporator to distribute the cool air.

Refrigerants

For every refrigerant there is a specific boiling, or vaporization, temperature associated with each pressure, so it is only necessary to control the pressure in the evaporator to obtain a desired temperature. A similar pressure-temperature relationship holds in the condenser. One of the most widely used refrigerants for many years has been dichlorodifluoromethane, known popularly as Refrigerant-12. This synthetic chlorofluorocarbon (CFC) when used as a refrigerant would, for example, vaporize at 20°F in its evaporator under a pressure of 35.7 psi, and after compression to 131.9 psi would condense at 100° F in the condenser. The resulting condensed liquid would then enter the expansion valve to drop to evaporator pressure and repeat the cycle of absorbing heat at low temperature and low pressure and dissipating heat at the much higher condenser pressure and temperature.

In small domestic refrigerators used for food storage, the condenser heat is dissipated into the kitchen or other room housing the refrigerator. With air-conditioning units the condenser heat must be dissipated out of doors or directly into cooling water. The biggest single problem in designing a cooling system for conversions is the problem of disposing of the heat extracted from the coach. It is essential to dump the heat from the condenser over board so that it may not be reingested by the condenser. After 1995 Freon-12 will no longer be manufactured. Currently, coach manufacturers are charging their air conditioning systems with Freon-22, which requires hard plumbing. A new refrigerant designated R-134a will replace all R-12, and contains no fluorocarbons. This refrigerant will be installed on all future vehicles.

Absorption System

A few household units and most RV refrigerators operate on the absorption principle. In such gas refrigerators a strong solution of ammonia in water is heated by a gas flame in a container called a generator, and the ammonia is driven off as a vapor which passes into a condenser. Changed to a liquid state in the condenser, the ammonia flows to the evaporator as in the compression system. Instead of the gas being inducted into a compressor on exit from the evaporator, however, the ammonia gas is reabsorbed into the partially cooled, weak solution returning from the generator, to form the strong ammonia solution. This process of reabsorption occurs in a container called the absorber, from which the enriched liquid flows back to the generator to complete the cycle.

Increasing use of absorption refrigeration now occurs in refrigeration units for comfort space cooling, for which purpose refrigerant temperatures of 45° to 50° F are suitable. In this temperature range, water can be used as a refrigerant with an aqueous salt solution, usually lithium bromide, as the absorbent material. The very cold boiling water from the evaporator is absorbed into a concentrated salt solution. This solution is then pumped into the generator, where, at an elevated temperature, the

Air Conditioning

surplus water is boiled off to increase the salt concentration of the solution; this solution, after cooling, recirculates back to the absorber to complete the cycle. The system operates at high vacuum with an evaporator pressure of about 0.145 psi; the generator and condenser operate at about 1.45 psi. The units are usually direct-fired or use steam generated in a boiler. These units are still available for residential application and go under the trade name Servel.

Central Air Conditioning System

Coleman manufactures a central air conditioning system which mounts out of sight, either on or under the floor of the coach. It is controlled by a wall thermostat and uses a system of ducts. The 2-Ton PLUS is basically two units in a single package. With moderate temperatures only one compressor is used, but when the temperature goes up, a second compressor kicks in.

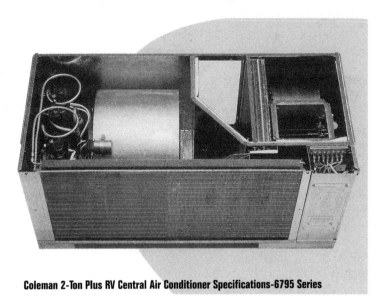

Coleman 2-Ton Plus RV Central Air Conditioner Specifications-6795 Series

Coleman claims with only one compressor in use, the system provides 20 percent more cooling than a comparable roof top unit, and 16 percent more with both compressors on compared with two rooftop units. They claim an airflow of twice that comparable to rooftop units. A significant advantage is a self-contained system without the need for pre-charged lines which may leak coolant. It may be located at any convenient place in the coach as long as it is adjacent to an outside wall, so as to permit the heat gathered in the condenser to exhaust to the outside. The condenser opening is approximately 15 x 33 inches. Properly designed duct work is essential for effective operation. Ducts should be sized per the manual and located as recommended. The unit occupies a space of 16½ x 21 x 44 inches.

Split Air Conditioning Systems

Split units are so named because they separate the compressor and condenser from the evaporator and fan as two separate units. This is similar to residential systems in which the compressor and condenser are normally placed outside the house, while the evaporator and blower reside inside the building. In a similar fashion, the split units are separated, so the fan and evaporator may be installed in an overhead cabinet with its small blower or fan. The compressor and condenser are then placed in the baggage compartment and are ventilated in such a manner the heat extracted from the condenser is dumped overboard or outside the coach. It is important the exhaust air passing through the condenser is removed from the compartment in a way that it cannot be re-ingested by the blower delivering air to the condenser. If this condition exists, the refrigeration process will be severely limited, since the whole process is one of extracting heat from the

Air Conditioning

living area and exhausting it to the outside. This is one of the reason air conditioning systems tend to loose their effectiveness as the outside temperature increases.

Another physical process occurring during the refrigeration cycle is the condensation of ambient air in the living quarters. This condensation occurs when the inside air passes over the cooling coils, (the evaporator). The moisture contained in the inside air contains a normal saturation point at the existing temperature. As it passes over the chilled coils, the saturated air drops below its dew point (condensation temperature). This causes the moisture in the air to liquefy, on the cooling coils creating condensation. A collection pan is normally designed into the evaporator section with a stub tube so a drain tube may be attached and allow the condensation water to drain overboard.

Several split units are customarily placed at strategic locations throughout the coach. Normally these units are available in ratings of 8,000 to 12,000 Btus, so they may be designed to create a selective cooling system, i.e., they may be located in such a manner to employ your electrical power to the most advantageous usage. Again, it is important to stress the effectiveness of a refrigerated cooling system is its ability to dispel the heat extracted from the cooled space.

Split units are made so they are pre-charged with refrigerant at the factory. They are connected with pre-charged lines. These lines are soft copper for flexibility, and have end fittings so they can be connected at each end. The ends are pierced to allow the coolant to move between each component. In addition, the lower component (the condenser/compressor unit) has schrader type valves (similar to the inflation valves on tires),so at any time the system needs charging it may be done by an independent refrigeration technician.

Split units are not uncommon and were originally developed for the mobile home industry. Many mobile home and RV supply companies market these systems.

Roof Air Conditioning Units

Roof air conditioning units are the most common in the R.V. industry. For one thing, they are relatively inexpensive, and are self contained. They easily and effectively get rid if the condenser heat, and are quite satisfactory in performance. In addition, they are easy to install, and in a worst case scenario, they are simply replaced. Roof-airs are installed over a standard 14-inch square opening. It is important to frame in the opening through the roof, especially if you cut through the roof center longeron. This framing should be welded in place and extend to the adjacent roof frames and longerons in order to distribute the loading. The only additional requirement is 12-gage 120VAC wiring. Roof air conditioners are now being made in units up to 15,000 Btus, so two or three units should cool a conversion adequately.

Air Conditioning

The roof A/C unit may also be remotely controlled with a thermostat. The Coleman company makes available a remote control unit which may be connected to their standard roof units. This allows the use of a ceiling fixture, which may be combined with lighting designed to conceal the normal roof A/C interior unit. Some quite dazzling ceiling fixtures have been installed in some conversions.

The most disagreeable feature of the roof air conditioning unit is the sound level of the blower delivering cooled air to the interior. For those of you sensitive to excessive noise levels, other solutions should be sought. Not only does the blower create a lot of noise, but the compressor, even the rotary type, contributes to the unpleasant noise factor.

Another drawback to the roof air conditioning unit is the external appearance. Some liken its appearance to a window air conditioning unit, but instead of sticking out of a window, it is sticking out of the roof. In some conversions, this may also be hazardous by causing an over-height condition. When you consider that the average floor height of a conversion is nearly five feet from the ground, then add another seven feet of interior height and structure, we are very close to 12 feet of height without any roof protuberances. If roof air conditioning units are employed, it is a wise practice to check the clearance of every underpass you come to. This is especially true back east.

I recall one time I was lost in New Bedford, Mass., and a courteous gentleman offered to lead me out of town. The first underpass he went through had a ten foot clearance, so I continued another block and found an underpass with a 13'-6" clearance. Fortunately, my guide came back and led me out of town to I-95. Our personal coach has an overall height of 12'-6".

We have the roof airs extending nine inches above the roof. The new 15,000 Btu units are 12 inches in height

Other Options

Another form of air conditioning which should be mentioned is the least expensive type, the common window air conditioner. Although this type of unit is not recommended for coach conversions, I have seen some clever modifications and installations of this system. The principal problem is that the window A/C is designed to eliminate condenser heat through natural convection into the outside air, and with a conversion, we don't have the luxury of protuberances sticking out of our normal contour. In addition to spoiling the beauty of the coach, it increases our aerodynamic drag and exceeds the allowable width limit by law. The installations I have seen create a large plenum inside the coach to exhaust the heat, and bring the make-up air from another source, such as a wheel well. This permits the complete unit to remain inside of the original coach contour. Again, I would discourage anyone from using this type of cooler, since it requires considerable innovation, occupies more space than necessary, and may, or may not work.

Heat Pumps

Although Cruisair could fit into the split air category, it is the only system I am currently aware of which can also be ordered as a heat pump. Hence, it is presented in the heat pump category.

The Cruisair total comfort system gives you great flexibility in directing airflow throughout the coach. A single condensing unit can support more than one cooling/heating unit, and

Air Conditioning

air can be ducted from a single cooling/heating unit to two separate areas. Cruisair's Applications Engineering Department renders assistance in laying out and specifying the best system for a given coach. Cruisair systems are available for cooling only or for

heating and cooling. The combined cooling/heating system works just like a home-type heat pump. The system contains a reversing valve which permits the condensing unit to function as a heat pump extracting ambient heat from the outside air. The reversing valve is controlled by the cabin switch assembly and provides for automatic changeover between the cooling and heating modes to maintain the thermostat setpoint. The Cruisair heat pump provides heating efficiency at outside temperatures down to 40 degrees F. For regular use in very cold temperatures, auxiliary duct heat-modules can be installed to provide warm airflow using the same ducts and grills as the air conditioning system. A variety of auxiliary heating options are available, and Cruisair Applications Engineers can help you choose. Condensing units are available in 14,000 BTU/hr models. The units are hermetically sealed for safe operation. Ventilation is required for the air-cooled refrigerant condenser, but the unit is not affected by moisture or vibration. Condensing units use fans or squirrel-cage blowers to move air across the coil. Blower models normally take air in through the coil in front and discharge it through the bottom of the unit. Fan-type units take air in the back and discharge it through the coil in front.

All Cruisair motor coach air conditioning systems are designed for 115V single-phase 60 Hz power, but 230V systems can be built on special order.

For more information on Cruisair products, including central air conditioners, contact **AAP**, Incorporated, P.O. Box 430, Milford, VA 22514, 1-(804)633-9454 or 7053 Cottontail St., Ventura, CA 93004 1-(800)647-7252.

Chapter Thirty Three

Summary

We have discussed heating, ventilating, and air conditioning of converted coaches, and many options have been presented. At this point in our discussion, it is time to summarize all we have learned and try to make a little sense of it. Presented are a set of tables rating the various systems and equipment by cost, comfort, efficiency and appearance. Keep in mind the ratings are those of the writer and your own rating may not necessarily agree. Included at the end of this section is a blank rating sheet for the use of each reader to help them choose the optimum system according to their circumstances. For simplicity, my rating system is based on a score of one to ten. For example, a high cost factor would rate low, along with a difficult installation. Naturally, good efficiency and attractiveness would rate high.

First, lets us summarize the cost and installation complexity of each system in a very broad manner. The Webasco and ProHeat systems cost in the neighborhood of $3,000 and up, depending on the number of radiator units selected. A rather sophisticated plumbing system is required, plus pressure testing. So the installation can be somewhat involved, requiring a talented technician. The Primus system can be as involved as the Webasco/AquaHot, and the cost is comparable. The primary difference is the Primus system uses propane for fuel. The forced-air heating system costs about $300 or more for the unit, plus the installation of the propane circuitry and the duct work. The installation of the forced air system can be extremely simple to mildly complex, depending on the duct work desired. The catalytic heaters cost in the range of $200 to $500 dollars per unit, are easy to install, but occupies precious wall space. The electric toe-kick style heater cost about $150 per unit, and is the easiest system to install, takes up no premium space, and may be wired into a 120VAC circuit. Obviously, if you plan to use the electric heater system, its power could be designed to utilize a thermostatic control for convenience.

With respect to ventilating devices, the after-market moonroof will cost about $300. The Fantastic Vents will run the gamut between $150 to $600, and the AlumaCool, and Koolamatic fans are in the $200 to $300 neighborhood. Custom windows for coach conversions are available from about $150 dollars and up. The Peninsula Glass company in Vancouver Washington fabricate a custom dual pane window for converted coaches for a little over $300 and up. All the custom windows mentioned are sliders with screens, and are easily installed by any conversion company, or yourself. Awnings are available from a number of manufacturers and range from about $300 per window to a full patio awning on the order of $800 to over $2,000. Noticeably, the numbers I have quoted are quite a broad brush, and hoping that inflation stays in check for a while, they should be in the ball park.

Air conditioning units range from about $600-$700 for the standard roof air to a similar figure for a standard split air from many mobile home supply companies. CruiseAir, originally developed for the yachting industry, have traditionally run about $1,500 dollars per unit. CruiseAir includes application engineering with their prices.

For a total system of heating, ventilating, and air conditioning on the economy scale, the prospective coach owner should budget about $6,000 which will include heating, openable windows, awnings, and air conditioning. To include a good diesel fired generator, add about $5,000. For a top of the line installation, $20,000 would not be out of line.

It may be noted in comparing the heating systems, no effort was made to segregate the diesel powered systems from the propane, or electric systems. If a specific form of fuel is mandatory for

Summary: Heating and Air Conditioning

your conversion, you should concentrate only on those systems falling within those parameters. As may be seen from the authors analysis, almost all the heating systems came out with the same score. But, this is purely a subjective rating (and a diplomatic presentation), yet the readers ratings may be entirely different. It may be revealed that the authors coach is heated with two 6,000 Btu catalytic heaters, plus four electric toe-kick heaters, yielding a total heating capacity of 27,600 Btus. Although this appears to be a mix and match system employing both propane and electric, it works for us.

Comparison Table, Heating Equipment

Equip	Cost	Installation	Efficiency	Looks	Score
Webasco	3	2	9	9	23
AquaHot	3	2	9	9	23
Primus	3	2	9	9	23
Forced Air	8	5	4	6	23
Catalytic	6	6	9	2	23
Electric	4	8	8	7	23

Comparison Table, A/C Equipment

Equip	Cost	Installation	Efficiency	Looks	Score
Central A/C	3	5	7	8	21
Split A/C units	2	3	7	8	21
Roof A/C units	8	8	5	0	21
Window A/C units	9	2	3	3	17

With regard to air conditioning systems, since no absorption units are available, and all the options are powered by electricity, this makes for an easier analysis. Keep in mind this book is designed to acquaint the prospective conversion owner, as to what is currently on the market. And the reader should rely heavily on his conversion specialist, and/or vendor specialists.

	System	System
	_____	_____
Cost	_____	_____
Installation	_____	_____
Efficiency	_____	_____
Appearance	_____	_____
Score	_____	_____

Part Five

Interior Design

The Bus Converter's Bible

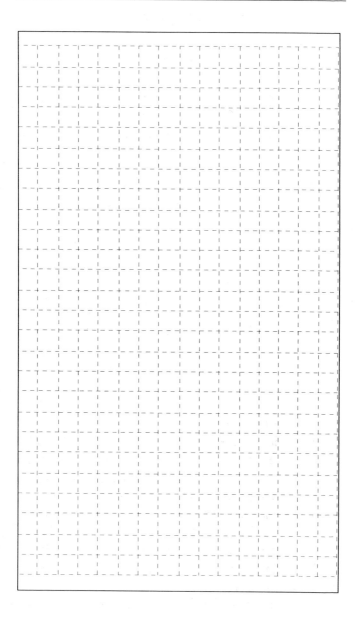

Chapter Thirty Four

Floor Plans

The subject of floor plans may seem a little out of place, since they are almost the first thing a person thinks about when starting a conversion. So, if my readers decided to jump ahead to this chapter before the rest, they are forgiven.

When drawing floor plans, it is suggested you use a scale of three-quarter inch to the foot. With this scale each one-sixteenth of an inch equals one inch on the coach. In addition, when laying out your design on your bus floor, it is advisable to use inches throughout for all your furniture, fixtures, appliances and equipment. Of course, if you've a European bent and wish to use millimeters, you may. Then your bus would be approximately 12,192 mm. in length. One time I had to design a machine in the metric system- - -drove me round the bend! (This may explains a lot!?)

For those of you with a computer, many of the CAD programs available today are ideal to develop your plans, since you may draw them out on the video screen, print them, and modify them with just a few key strokes. And these CAD (Computer Aided Design) programs have become reasonable in price.

As for the basic dimensions, the average 96-inch wide coach will generally yield about 91 inches of interior width. This will depend, of course, on how thick you make the interior side walls, and the wall coverings. In the case of the Eagle coach, keep in mind from the window sill level to the beginning of the roof bows, the width becomes one inch narrower. For example, if with your side walls covered, you have an inside width at the floor line of 90½ inches, your inside width near your window headers will be 89½ inches. The inside width of the average 102-inch wide coach will reflect the same sort of reduction.

The length of the flat floor of an Eagle is 399 inches from

the bulkhead behind the drivers seat to the step just before the air cleaner housing. Every brand of bus is slightly different. Just keep in mine if you figure everything to the nearest inch, even with tolerance build-ups, a little shaving here and there, you will still be able to make every thing fit.

A few standard items have the following dimensions:

Item	Size
Queen size bed	60 .. x . 80
Lavatory front to splash	 19
Toilet drain out from wall	 12
Passage door width	21 .. to . 22
Ceiling vent opening	14 .. x . 14
Counter top width	 24
Counter top height	 36
Dining table height	29 .. to . 30
Window sill height	 30
Seating height	15 .. to . 17
Couch depth	 32
Std refrigerator width	 24
Side by Side Refrigerator	 32
Closet depth (minimum)	 21
Shower stall plan dims.	32 .. to . 38

Although the figures given above in inches are not cast in concrete, they will give the reader an idea of the space needed to provide a livable design.

It is a good idea to superimpose the upper floor plan over the lower baggage section along with the location of the wheels and engine. This way the interferences can be predicted and solved before they become a major problem.

The tankage, such as fresh water, and holding tanks should be layed-out so you know how to route your plumbing. The formula for tankage is L x W x H / 231 equals gallons. In simpler terms 231 cubic inches equal one U.S.gallon.

The drawing shown on the next page is a typical side aisle layout. There is no one best plan; this is what makes the individual bus conversion so interesting. One of the more functional designs is to install the bathroom at the very rear of the coach. Since the rear of most buses are occupied with mechanical and engine type things, often about two feet of the rear of the coach is lost for floor planning. By installing the bathroom in the rear, using this two feet as part of the vanity and lavatory, the overall length gain in living space is two feet. This design lends itself to separate twin beds on either side of the aisle od a full size or queen bed made be installed laterally with the head placed at either side of the coach.

One problem with installing the bathroom at the rear of the coach is the black water tank will probably have to be installed with a macerator pump to transfer the contents to a forward holding tank, or simply install a larger black water tank. There is no problem routing the shower and lavatory waste water to a forward holding tank.

Keep in mind when designing your floor plan the placement of the windows. For example: the kitchen windows behind the counter top. If you plan to have a window there, its sill height should be at least 40 inches. The normal window sill height is 30 inches. If various window heights are used, it is customary to maintain a constant header height for uniform appearance. Also, when selecting your window locations keep in mind the location of a patio awning, and/or window awnings.

Keep your design simple. Avoid jutting countertops, angular sink placement, and joggled hallways. Also, avoid opening doors into cabinets and other obstructions. Remember a refrigerator does not have a sliding door and must open into the room area where the occupant may have to stoop to inspect the contents.

The Bus Converter's Bible

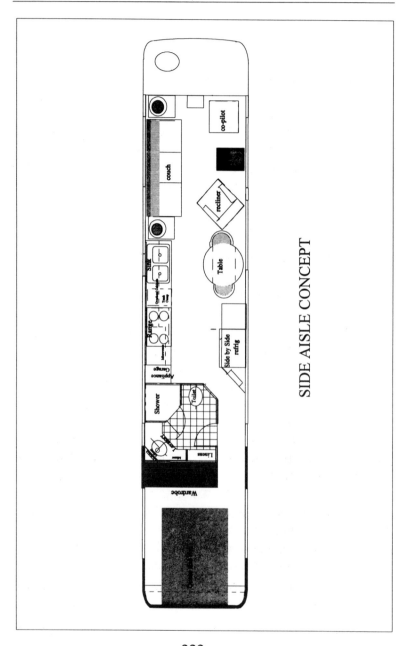

Consider the installation of a roof deck with collapsible rails and a pop-up awing for sporting event viewing, and just plain scenery enjoyment. An inside wall mounted ladder will be necessary for this along with an escape hatch of at least 22 inches square. This could be incorporated into a moonroof installation.

The incorporation of a washer and dryer is seldom a good idea unless you want to wash almost every day. However, they are made for the RV trade with minumal capacity; approximately a five pound load. The principle drawback is you must carry enough water to cycle a wash load or you must be hooked up. If you are hooked up, chances are you are in a park where washer/dryers are available. No doubt, these small units are useful in a pinch.

A Trash compactor which measures only 12 inches wide has been marketed for years by Montgomery Ward. Recently, Dometic has begun to market a similar size unit. We have had one for years and we like it.

In the past, unless you had an all electric coach, a separate ice maker was almost a necessity. The most common size of the U-line brand and also the Dometic is 14 inches wide by 24 inches high. Recently Dometic is also marketing a side by side refrigerator with a built-in ice maker. The complete unit measures only 32 inch wide.

In many cases it is a good idea to pre-purchase the appliances you plan to install, Then you may take the exact measurements from the units. In case you are not be sure what you want to install, just go to the supplier and measure the largest type of machine you might use and plan to accommodate it. If you select a smaller unit later, the cabinet work may then be adjusted.

When designing your floor plan, keep in mind any duct work you may wish to install and be sure to plan for plumbing runs and wire chases. A favorite location for wiring is above the window headers, since the windows will have blinds, curtains, and/or valances to hide any conduits. Another logical location is along the baseboards. Recently many raised roof coaches have been elevated to the degree that air conditioning duct work can be included in a double ceiling. This has the benefit of providing additional insulation. Furnaces may logically be installed in the baggage compartment, then have the heat ducted to a strategic location along the baseboard or, for example, into the floor of the bathroom.

    It is a good idea when preparing your floor plan to generate separate overlays which may be done easily using a computer CAD program. The purpose of the overlays is to create a floor plan, a mechanical plan, a plumbing plan, and an electrical plan, each separately. Also included would be an overlay of the baggage compartment which relates to the specific overlay plan. The overlay approach may still be done the old fashioned way; using tracing paper, or onion skin. Or pick up some quadrille pads at the stationary store. They are marked in grids at every quarter-inch.

    As a final approach, after you are satisfied with your plan, tape it onto the floor of your coach spray paint the tape, then strip the tape. Walk around the plan in full size, place boxes or other things where various items are going to be to see if it works for you. Try to create a full size three dimensional effect. Have your beloved also change it around to satisfy her (or him).

Chapter Thirty Five

Walls and Bulkheads

Walls and bulkheads are simply defined as those items that separate different living functions, and the side wall materials. Cabinets may be incorporated as bulkheads if, for example, they separate the kitchen from the bathroom. But for the most part, the reason for discussing walls and bulkheads separately from cabinets is different treatments and materials.

Also, in this discussion, we will include the sub-headliner, which is the material applied directly under the framework, or furring strips. Earlier we spoke of insulation, but we must consider what is under the insulation in the overhead structure. Furring strips are customarily applied directly to the frame of the coach. A minimum spacing of 8 inches side to side is recommended for 1 x 2 furring strips. This allows the builder to work in multiples of standard material widths. The recommended sub-headliner base is ¼ inch thick plywood. Along the sides of the coach, two thicknesses of ⅛ inch door skins, or plywood may be used to achieve the sharp bend at the edges. Also, bender board plywood is available in which the grain all runs one direction. This material is designed to make radical bends, such as are at the roof-side transitions of a bus.

The interior side walls of the coach frame are generally covered with at least ⅜-inch plywood. However, I have seen some builders use ¾-inch plywood. The simple attachment technique is to use *Tec* screws through the plywood into the steel framework of the bus. These are screws with self drilling tips and will penetrate up to about 0.080 thick steel. A somewhat less expensive approach is to use # 6 drywall screws, by drilling an ⅛-inch diameter pilot hole through both the material and the steel frame. Using two drill motors, one with the drill bit and one with a Phillips driver bit, the job goes quite fast and smoothly.

When installing either furring strips or overhead plywood, use a couple of sticks a little longer than the height of the ceiling as props to hold the material overhead, then it becomes a one man job.

When installing bulkheads, use a good quality of ¾-inch plywood. You may plan to cover it with laminate later. Otherwise use a good grade of hardwood plywood which you may complete with a natural finish. I have seen builders lay down miniature plates, studs and headers, and sheath the interior walls with a thinner plywood. The principle reason for doing this is to conceal wiring and place switches inside the walls. By carefully considering your wiring and switch location, this may be avoided by installing the wiring and switches inside of various cabinets. For example, a hall switch to a bathroom light may be placed inside a linen cupboard for concealment. Since there is no framework to attach the bulkheads, plan to use 1 x 2 cleats attached to the floor and ceiling. Another technique is to use clip angles screwed to both the floor and the bulkheads. Again, through judicious planning, these cleats, or clip angles, may be concealed inside of cabinets and cupboards.

Because of the high cost of materials, it has recently become acceptable to employ manufactured panel products, such as wafer board. Although wafer board is somewhat ugly, due to its dimensional stability it lends itself to covering with plastic laminate, such as Formica. This is also true of particle board. If either of these materials become wet, however, they expand and tend to come unglued. As far as the new wafer boards, it has become common practice to make weather siding for residential construction in the Northwest, so there must be an immense improvement in the adhesive use to manufacture this product.

For use in determining how many screws should be used for both wall and cabinet installation, the following chart is provided for your consideration.

Screw Pullout Load in Pounds with 3/4-inch Penetration

Size	Diam.	Fir	Oak	Walnut
#6	.138	74	188	106
#7	.151	80	206	116
#8	.164	88	224	126
#10	.190	101	260	146

The values shown in the table above are based on average values of the specific gravity of the wood listed. These numbers can vary plus, or minus at least twenty percent due to a lower density factor of the wood used.

The way I would use this table, if I were installing a cabinet to the overhead, is to figure the weight of the cabinet, use a load factor of four (impact factor= 2 times a safety factor=2), then use enough screws to overcompensate by at least 50 percent. As an example: an 80 pound cabinet x 4 = 320 pound load. Supported by the fir furring strips with number six screws, I would use at least eight screws. Then I could go over the roughest road I came to, and the cabinet would hang on!

The Bus Converter's Bible

Notes:

Sketches

Chapter Thirty Six

Headliners

Headliners are one of the items that tend to give your coach the warm, finished look and feel. There is no hard and fast rule for headliners, only that they have a professional appearance. Headliners are often a fine carpet like material, but they have been as simple as a good grade of wall paper. Vinyl, Naugahyde style fabric has been used for years along with a form of felt, or velvet type material. It was even popular several years ago to use a bamboo style wall paper.

The headliner is applied to a substrate, which must be installed first. This substrate, or base is generally ¼-inch plywood applied to furring strips. On the bare framework of the coach, I suggest 1 x 2 furring strips be screwed in place. A typical method of attaching the furring strips is with 1½ x #8 Tec screws (these are the screws with a drill point on the end, so they drill their own hole). Another approach is to drill through the furring strip with an ⅛-inch diameter drill and fasten the furring strip with #6 drywall screws.

The preferred spacing of the furring strips is 8 inches on center. This allows a center section of a full width of 4-foot-wide plywood to occupy the middle of the coach ceiling where the contour is at a minimum. In addition, by using a multiple of 8 inches, after the plywood section is in place, the location of the furring strips can be determined for future cabinet hanging. At the edges, two laminates of ⅛-inch thick plywood may be bent into the corners. Although my recommendation is to use ¼-inch ceiling base, you may use anything which makes you feel good. For example, some builders would prefer to use a ceiling base ½-inch thick, so that they might hang their cabinets without worrying if they penetrate a furring strip with their cabinet fasteners. This is the choice of the builder. I simply recommend a minimum of ¼-inch material.

One advantage of applying the furring strips is it permits one to route wiring between the furring strips. In addition, the insulated roof section has been increased by another ¾ inches, providing more of a heat barrier. After the ceiling base is installed, the builder is ready to apply the headliner.

Prior to installing the headliner, pre-install your overhead cabinets temporarily. While they are up, mark around them, and add strips of uniform thickness approximately ⅛-inch away from the face of the cabinets. These strips may be plywood or other strips of wood. They should be at least ¼-inch thick. Then fill in the spaces outside the cabinet area between the strips with your foam padding. The cabinets are then removed for finishing. The next thing to do is apply your finished headliner, allowing the material to continue over the strips and into the inside of the cabinet area. Using this approach, when you re-install your cabinets permanently, the cabinets will tuck up inside these strips providing a completely finished appearance without the need to add any molding, plus the interior of all the cabinets will be lined with your headliner material, and fit the finished contour perfectly.

The padding noted above is a sub-headliner which is often applied in the form of a closed cell flexible foam. This foam tends to bridge many surface imperfections, and soften the final headliner. It is applied with a spray type contact adhesive. The adhesive is available at most automotive upholstery suppliers as Landau roof contact adhesive. It is readily thinned and sprayed through an inexpensive paint gun.

Perhaps the most common headliner is a thin carpet like material manufactured by Ozite Corporation of Libertyville, Illinois. This material is made from polypropylene, the same kind of plastic used for floating ski ropes. It is felted with an embossed pattern, much like the paper manufacturing process. It can be molded over simple contours, and is almost inert to all forms of solvent. It is applied with a spray type contact adhesive, applying the glue to both surfaces then rolling into place.

The material may be purchased in widths of 54, 72 and 96 inches. Since the material has the ability to warp, the following technique is recommended for installing this material in a uniform manner. Assume you wish to apply the material laterally across the coach from one window sill height to the other window sill level. Fabricate a temporary saw horse frame which nearly touches the ceiling of the bus. Then drape the material across the saw horse centering the material both on the saw horse and in the middle of the coach. From this position, spray adhesive is applied to both the material and the ceiling in a band width about 1 to 2 feet. The material is then carefully lifted by the saw horse to touch the ceiling, where it sticks. It is then carefully patted out and smoothed, avoiding any warping. The material is now hanging from the ceiling and adhesive is applied again in about a 1 to 2 foot width band. The material is smoothed in place, and the process is continued until one side is finished. The process is repeated on the other side until the material is completed from side to side. Continue the process in material widths until the coach is completed. A razor knife is used to trim the material, and the edges will be hidden with cabinets, valences, or trim.

A technique to trim between the lateral bands of headliner material is to use the old fashioned process of wood bending. A steam box is fabricated from redwood using a 5 gallon drum of water about half full and heated by a propane shop heater. Strips of oak, $3/8 \times 1\frac{1}{2}$ inches by about 10 feet long are steamed for about 15 minutes. These hot strips are handled with gloves and bent and clamped around a plywood form, then allowed to cool and dry. Holes are cut out of the form to allow the clamps to engage, and the form is exaggerated in contour to allow spring-back after the clamps are removed. The bent strips are then edge shaped with a router, and sanded. The strips are installed with screws and the screw holes are plugged and sanded before finishing..

Vinyl fabric is normally applied using the tuck and roll process. This a technique where one lateral strip of vinyl fabric is stapled to the overhead base, then folded back over itself, stretched, and stapled again. Then the next piece is repeated in the same pattern. The illustration below shows one process.

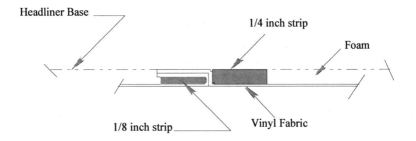

Cross section thru Headliner Tuck and Roll concept

Chapter Thirty Seven

Window Dressing

What do you do with bus windows? Should you keep the original bus windows, or install RV style windows with screens and sliders? The answer to a lot of these questions depends on the way you plan to convert your coach.

By all means, it is preferable to have sliding windows for a conversion, unless you plan to provide continuous air conditioning with filtered air. Sliding windows demand screens to keep out insects.

RV style windows, ie., sliders with screens, are available from several manufacturers. They will make your windows to order to fit the opening of a specific coach such as a GMC, an MCI, an Eagle, or what ever make you have. Some of these fabricators are: Peninsula Glass in Vancouver, WA, Hehr in Los Angeles, and Kinro in Mira Loma, CA, and Texas.

Another source for windows are RV surplus stores. These surplus windows are new, but the chances of actually finding window to fit you coach are almost nil. However, if you are willing to accept windows which will require some custom framing for installation, these windows are quite acceptable. The savings can be as much a eighty percent over custom made windows.

Smaller windows in height are called for behind the kitchen counter, and one certainly would not want full size windows in the bathroom. So it may be to your advantage to shop the surplus yards for this sort of thing.

Windows may be installed by applying a sealant material to the inside of the outside flanges, then laying them in the opening, installing a retaining ring from the inside and attaching with screws. This sort of installation sandwiches the body of the coach between the outside flange and the retaining ring flange. This inside retaining ring also goes by the name of *beauty ring*, or *hooty ring*.

Another way to install the window is to simply screw, or rivet the window flange to the siding, or coach body. Be sure to apply sealant before placing the window into the opening. Many sealants are acceptable, and inexpensive. The least expensive sealant is the common butyl rubber, often called *tub and tile sealer*. This material will accept paint and cleans up with water before it cures. Silicone rubber is not recommended because it contaminates any surface it touches with a release agent and paint will not stick to it. The old fashioned *putty tape* should be avoided for the same reason, although a diligent cleaning with solvent around the area will minimize the contamination. The best sealant available would be a urethane elastomer, such as *Sikaflex* or a 3M product. They are some what expensive.

Now that your windows are installed, what sort of treatment do you provide for the inside? The solution to this problem has many answers. It is limited only to your imagination. The simplest, though not the most attractive solution is to allow the *beauty ring* to be exposed, laying on the interior wall treatment. If a retaining ring is not used, and a plastic laminate is applied to the interior walls, the laminate may be used to line the inside of the window ledges. If shadow boxes are planned, the support bases may be applied to the walls and no additional treatment may be needed other than the retaining ring, since with the shades, or blinds in place, no unsightly areas will be exposed.

It is strongly recommended valances be installed over each window, or set of windows, since this is a natural conduit for routing mechanical items such are wiring or ductwork. Furthermore, all blinds, shades, drapes, or other window treatment demand valances. These valances may be any material which coordinates your interior, such as hardwood, laminate or padded fabric.

The actual shades, blinds, drapes or window covers are you choice. Some of the items used in the past are mini-blinds. The principle drawback to mini-blinds are their inclination to collect dust. Special brushes have been made to clean these blinds, but they are not very effective. Recently a pleated blind has come into favor, known as the *Day/Night* blind. This blind uses two blinds with a sheer material on the bottom and an opaque material which may be pulled down after the sheer section. The blind is secured with guide strings in tension at each side so either section will remain where they are left. Finally, the old fashioned drape is pretty hard to beat when it comes to elegance. These may be further enhanced by motorized drapery rods. Keep in mind, almost anything you can install in a home may be adapted to a motorcoach.

The Bus Converter's Bible

Notes:

Sketches

Chapter Thirty Eight

Cabinets

Most people believe the major portion of a conversion is the cabinet work. As may be seen from this book, it is a relatively small part of the conversion. However, it is without a doubt the most visible, and striking part of the conversion process.

The cabinets may be fabricated the old fashioned way using good furniture manufacturing techniques. They may also be built in a myriad of radical ways. I have seen cabinets in coaches framed with welded steel tubing hung from the coach framework. Obviously, the converter did not want the cabinets to fall from the ceiling as the coach traveled down the road. Although this is certainly a fail-safe approach to hanging cabinets it is probably what one might call an *over-kill*.

The conventional technique for fabricating cabinets is to make a carcass, fabricate a face-frame using dowels, screws, or biscuits, attach the face-frame with glue and staples, or finishing nails, and then have the doors made by a company specializing in cabinet doors. The conventional cabinet carcass is made from hardwood plywood with the face-frame made from the matching hardwood. The most popular hardwoods are oak, walnut, maple, and ash.

The european style cabinets will normally be made from a manufactured material such as particle board, or chip board, then covered with a plastic laminate such as Formica, or Wilson Art. Often the european cabinet style will employ flush doors with concealed hinges. These cabinets are very plain with virtually no ornamental detail.

A variety of hinges for the cabinet doors are available. The most common is the exposed cabinet hinge available everywhere finished in a brass or antique bronze, and are made for both the rabbeted door and the surface mounted door. An attractive form of concealed hinge is the Youngsdale hinge. It too, is available in the rabbeted style and the surface mount. A popular style of hinge for RV application is the spring-loaded concealed hinge used to mount top hinged doors so the door remains open when opened. It is spring-loaded closed when closed. A technique for holding top hinged doors open using conventional hinges is to add a length of screen door spring as a prop. To close the door, simply deflect the spring and the door will close.

Often, it is advisable to add a false bottom to an overhead cabinet where you might wish to install an overhead lamp fixture or an electrical switch without penetrating the inside bottom of the cabinet with wires or electrical boxes.

The overhead contours of the coach sides must be accommodated by the cabinets. Several techniques are used to make templates to duplicate the contours. If the technique discussed earlier in the headline chapter is employed, the side contours do not have to be too precise. However it is a good idea to be as accurate as possible. One method is to secure a strip of thin wood near the ceiling. This may be made by ripping ⅛-inch plywood into about ¾-inch wide strips. Then, staple additional strips along this base strip radiating into the ceiling surface contour about an inch or so apart. After this is done, the assembly may be taken down and laid onto a piece of ⅛-inch thick plywood and a template cut to match the tips of the strips. The template may then be positioned to verify its shape, and modified where needed for precision. Other methods are to use cardboard, and cut and fit until satisfied.

Counter and table tops may be made from the base hardwood used to fabricate the cabinets. Another elegant choice is a solid acrylic plastic material, such as Corian, or Fountainhead. This material is a plastic material which is a uniform solid through out its thickness. It can be worked with standard woodworking tools. It can be joined to form an invisible joint, but requires a special adhesive which is the same chemistry as the basic material. In order to buy this material, the craftsman must complete a course in working with it. If you are confident of your talents, you might buy this solid top material from a cabinet shop, but it is advisable to have this project done by a specialist.

Tile counter-tops, contrary to popular opinion, will survive in a moving vehicle such as a bus conversion. New adhesives are now available which possess an elastic quality, and elastic grouts can be purchased. Tile may even be set with silicone and grouted with a butyl rubber compound, such as *tub and tile sealer*. However, conventional tile working techniques are applicable to conversions.

Drawer guides are almost as varied as the cabinets. The top of the line are the ball bearing full extension drawer guides made by *Accuride*, and *Grant*. Inexpensive drawer guides, such as are installed in inexpensive houses are available from most home improvement and hardware stores. The better guides must be ordered from cabinets specialty supply companies. An old fashioned technique is to rabbet the inside of the drawer cabinet, and to add strips of wood to each side of the drawers to slide in the grooves. The inverse, of course is another way of doing it, ie., grooving the drawer sides. Many antique cabinets have no drawer guides, but simply rely on the close fitting tolerances of the assemble. The antiques do employ cleats, or strips of wood at each side of the cabinets for the drawer to slide on.

Positive latching is a must in coach conversion cabinets, doors and drawers. Common friction catches are seldom up to the task. Several new forms of latching drawer knobs and pulls have recently come on the market. The yacht and marine industry have developed a number of ways to solve these problems. And, of course, the RV industry has developed some of their own methods. Since there is always something new on the horizon, no effort will be made to describe anything specific. Just keep in mind that slide bolts, hooks and latches are available.

Chapter Thirty Nine

Floor Treatment

The obvious treatment for floors is wall to wall carpet. However, other forms of flooring are ideal for bus conversions. Beginning with the entry way, consider ceramic tile. How, you may ask yourself, can ceramic tile survive in a moving vehicle, and, would it add too much weight? The answer is yes, and no. Tile is applied routinely to wooden floors and to the upstairs of homes. New adhesives are now available to bond tile to porous and to slick surfaces such as over old linoleum. Many bus conversions, for years, have carpeted the entry way . This carpet ultimately becomes soiled and ragged since it is the most used floor surface of the coach. And one doesn't have a chance to clean one's shoes before entering the coach in rainy weather, or at a dirty diesel fuel stop. Linoleum or vinyl tile would serve well, but this material being soft, finally becomes imbedded with sand, tiny pebbles and scuff marks. Rubber tile that is commonly used in many airports, would be quite appropriate for the entry steps. This material is quite expensive but obviously is made for very high traffic conditions.

Naturally, we would want a good grade of carpet in the living room and the bedroom of the coach. Often the carpet is applied to the walls up to the windows sill level. Since chairs tend to scuff the walls up to this level, the carpet protects both the chairs and the wall. Use a good grade of padding under the carpet and it will feel just like home. The carpet may be installed in the same manner as it is in your home with tack strips or it may be installed with a narrow crown staple, or both. It is strongly recommended that an experienced carpet layer install your carpet.

The kitchen and dinning area lends itself to the use of ceramic tile or marble, with throw rugs for warmth. Again, new adhesives and grout are available to bond the marble to a plywood base. Try to avoid Travertine marble, since it is as fragile as egg shells. The author installed Travertine in his personal coach because it was left over from his daughter's new house and although it still resides in the bathroom area, it has since been removed from the kitchen and dining areas. Granite marble tiles can be purchased which are tough and elegant. They may be bedded in an elastic thin-set mortar and will endure the motion of the coach without failure. Tile is easily cut and shaped with a diamond saw blade. Although these blades are very expensive, it more than pays for itself if you do the work yourself. Otherwise, have an experienced tile setter do your tile work.

Wood floors can be had in a variety of materials. Oak is the most common. In addition, pre-finished oak flooring material is readily available and made to be installed with mastic cement, staples, or finished nailers. In Oregon, a beautiful wood material made into flooring is myrtlewood. Pre-finished wood flooring comes in tiles of parquet design, and in pegged ranch design. One interesting floor pattern seen in a converted bus was a combination of oak ranch style strips, inset with a random pattern of Corian countertop fabricated tiles. Although the Corian tiles would tend to be scuffed, since they are a solid, homogeneous material, the color will always show through.

The type of flooring you choose is limited only by your imagination, your pocket book, and your talents. Select what feels good to you.

Part Six

Exterior Design

The Bus Converter's Bible

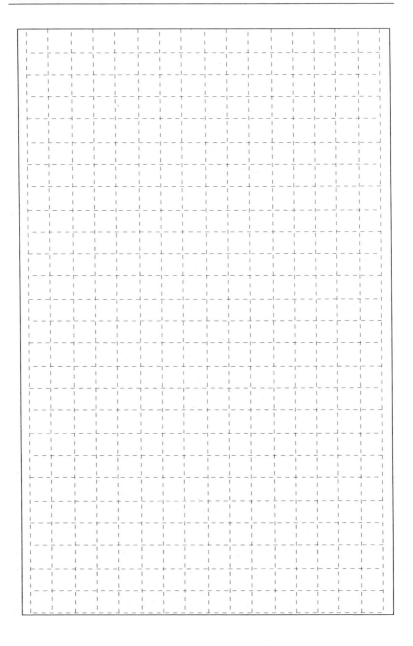

Chapter Forty

Body Work

The amount of body work needed on your coach before it is painted will vary with the age of the coach and its service. Obviously, a new coach should need no body work and it will probably already be painted, so if this is your situation, read no further.

Body work is a skill which requires a great deal of patience. The old fashioned leading process (melting lead in place), has been supplanted with the newer plastic processes. Bondo has become synonymous with body filler material, and is made up of polyester resin and clay. It is cured, or catalyzed with a peroxide, which is generally carried in a solvent such a MEK (methyl ethyl ketone). Often these catalysts will have a color so when mixed with the resin material, a certain hue will be evident and with experience, the worker will know just about how much time he has to work the material. If the mixture is made too hot, (too much catalyst), not only will the working time be limited, but the strength will be compromised. The amount of catalyst required will also very with the ambient temperature, or whether the mixture is being applied in the sun.

It is much better to apply the filler material in thin layers and built up to the contour slowly. The polyester material has the ability to bond to itself through the process called cross-linking. During the hardening process, each molecule reaches out and grabs the adjacent molecule until one giant molecule results. After the filler has begun to set up, it becomes a cheese like substance. It may be worked with a rasp like tool to approximate contour. This must be done carefully so as not to remove filler below the contour. Finally, after enough filler has been applied in thin layers, the surface may be rough sanded with a double-action sander. The process should be repeated with a smoothing putty, which has a finer grade of clay filler, and will sand as smooth as the body needs to be.

After bringing the repair to contour it should be primed with a sanding primer. This is a primer paint that may be sanded smooth and will fill tiny pin holes. Finish sanding should be with at least 220 grit and finally 440 grit sand paper. A technique used by professional body men is to slide the flat of their hand over the repair. Even when you cannot see a slight discontinuity, your hand is sensitive enough to detect it. If you think you may have finished a repair and it looks good to your eye, there will be a time when the sun or light is at a position which will reveal a blemish. Rely on your sense of touch, not your eyes.

When a repair is large enough or there is a gap or a large discontinuity, it will be necessary to reinforce the repair with glass fibers. Glass fibers come in many configurations. You may use mat, which is a felted type material with random oriented fibers approximately two inches long. Roving is a series of continuous glass fibers, similar to a rope, but without a twist. Glass fabric is a woven material with a basket type weave, ie., the fibers are oriented at ninety degrees to each other. And woven roving is a heavy fabric material woven like a basket weave using the glass roving. The strongest material for, say a boat hull, would be the woven roving. It also builds up in thickness faster. This would seldom be used in a body type repair unless there was severe damage.

The most common body material for reinforcement would be fiberglass mat. This is similar to material sprayed with a chopper gun with glass fibers 2 to 3 inches longs in a random pattern mat. It provides adequate reinforcement and is omnidirectional in strength. A useful tool when using mat is a washer roller. This is similar to a paint roller, but is made with a series of washers, approximately 1½-inch in diameter, and ½-inch diameter alternately stacked on a rod. This tool allows the mat fibers to be rolled and pushed down into the resin matrix. For example, if you paint the resin on the repair, and then apply the mat to the wet resin, it is sometimes difficult to wet out all the fibers with a brush. This is true even if you apply a second coat of resin. Use the washer roller over the repair and the resin and mat will be homogenized, but the roller will not pick up the glass fibers. After the repair is reinforced, it should then be finished to contour as described above.

If your bright metal, such as your silver sides or your aluminum is damaged, it will be necessary to replace the damaged part. There are a number of companies across the country which will sell you metal skin panels finished to size. Siding is available so you may cut and size it yourself. It is not my intention to name any firm which furnishes these products. They may readily be determined through various magazines ads.

The Bus Converter's Bible

Notes:

Sketches

Chapter Forty One

Prime Coats

P riming a coach prior to painting is not a very high level technical task. My apologies to those professionals reading these words. The main problem concerning priming a coach is to use the proper material, and do a careful job of masking.

Masking is a talent which simply takes patience, and the right materials. I hate to blow anyone's horn, but I personally, will only use masking tape made by Minnesota, Mining and Manufacturing (3M). There are other makers of masking tape which may be just as good, but this is a fetish with me. 3M masking tape has the capacity of lasting for several days, even in the sun, and still releasing from the surface without printing or vulcanizing. Cheaper tapes react to the ultraviolet spectrum of the sun becoming brittle, and bake onto the surface, requiring solvent cleanup. This will, unfortunately, remove the paint you just applied.

Masking paper may be purchased from any automotive paint supply company. A simple, inexpensive masking machine may be purchased from many tool outlet shops. It is nothing more than a stand with a mandrel for the paper and one for the tape which allows both to be removed simultaneously with half of the edge of the tape sticking to the edge of the paper. Then a serrated cutter allows one to tear off a strip of paper with the tape pre-stuck to one edge. The days of the newspaper for masking are over. Before using the masking paper, carefully go around each element with masking tape, making sure the edges are fully covered. Then the paper is used to finish covering the element.

For finished sharp and clean edges use fine line tape. This is a tape similar to electrician's vinyl tape, but much thinner.

When applied, this fine line tape will leave a clean sharp line, whereas the standard crepe paper masking tape will leave a ragged edge where the paint has bled through under the tape.

Carefully mask all of the areas of the coach not be painted, such as around windows and windshields. Any items which can be removed such as lamps or mirrors, should be. Also, remove any trim strips or molding, unless they are to be painted. If you have bright metal siding to be protected from paint, it should be wrapped with polyethylene film, especially if it is along the lower section of the coach, such as on an Eagle. This plastic is readily available from a garden supply shop or a home improvement store.

If the bus must be moved after it has been masked, simply cut a little window out of the paper in front of the windshield as shown in the photograph.

The primer paint may be shot with a cheap gun, which may be bought at a discount warehouse or discount tool outlet. The reason we can get by with inexpensive tools is that it is a one time operation for the reader. These cheap tools are copies of more expensive domestic built tools and some of them are really quite good.

The primer material is normally an acrylic lacquer base. Other primer materials may be an epoxy base or a urethane base. This is a subject where you should consult with a professional. Or you might consult with your automotive paint supplier. Sherwin-Williams probably has the most knowledgeable sales personnel, since S-W manufactures most of the industrial coating systems in the country. Other respected manufacturers are Pittsburgh Plate Glass and DuPont. The paint made by Sikkens, a Dutch company, has probably the biggest selection of colors available from any manufacturer.

The color of your primer should probably be a light grey. This primer color can successfully be covered and hidden by almost any finish color. The final prime coat should be a sanding primer. Sanding primer will fill pin holes, and may be finish sanded to an exceptionally smooth surface. It is suggested the final finish sanding be done by hand with number 440 grit, and then use the flat of the hand to test for any imperfections.

Notes:

Sketches

Chapter Forty Two

Graphics and Paint Systems

When we speak of graphics, we are talking about the various designs and patterns of colors of the paint job. Some people want a very simple paint job; others want a very elaborate color scheme. Murals or objects or scenery are also classified as graphics.

To execute a simple, but elegant color scheme, of say four colors, it may take five colors to do the job right. For example, it is often desirable to have a separating color between each of the major colors. This sometimes is done with tape, but a more professional job is done with paint.

Let us assume that we are planning a color scheme using the cool side of the color spectrum. This might be medium blue, light blue, lavender and rose (mauve). Regardless of the specific design layout, it would be desirable to separate these colors from each other with a different color. My choice would be silver, rather than a darker color such as black or red, but this is a matter of personal taste

The technique would be to paint the whole coach with the silver color. Then the graphics would be laid-out using a fine line tape, for example, one-half inch wide. Then the various colors would be painted and masked between. After the last color has been applied, the fine line tape would be stripped, leaving a silver margin, or separator, between each color. After that, a the clear glossy coat is applied over the coach. When the clear coat is completed, the separator lines almost look like tape, but they do not protrude above the surface contour as tape would.

3M manufacturers a variety of vinyl tapes in many colors and widths that are used for graphic design. Although the tape lays on the surface, it is quite thin and a skilled applier can make it look like a high-level paint job. This material is applied with water. What this means is that the surface of the bus must be smooth, and with its final finished color completed. Then, kept wet while the graphic tape is applied. This allows the tape to be adjusted, straightened, and aligned before it sets up on the surface. After the tape is in position, it may be sponged to remove excess water and then squeegeed to bring it down to the surface. The advantage of this system is minimal masking with the edges of the graphics being sharp and precise. The tape process may also be used as separator lines between colors as we discussed in the preceding paragraph. One advantage of doing it this way is that by using the graphics tape as a separator color, the masking between colors does not have to be as precise.

Another technique for doing graphics color separation is to build colors on top of colors. In this approach, we use our spray gun and spray a color along a stripe without any masking, making sure that we have sprayed over the area belonging to that color, and allowing it to fade out on each side of the target area. That stripe, or section, is then carefully masked with fine line tape and paper. Then we spray the next adjacent color, again without masking, and allowing it to fade to each side. The new section is then carefully masked, and we continue to apply as many colors as we wish using this technique. It is important when using this technique, to make sure that the masking tape does not lift the newly applied paint. This can be assured by following the manufacturer's recommendations. With most urethane based base coats, they may be taped over in about thirty minutes after application without being lifted by subsequent masking.

This brings us to the various paint systems for automotive

painting. Almost all the new cars built today use a urethane paint system, sometimes called a polyurethane process. The older more common automotive paints are acrylic enamels, which may, or may not be catalyzed.

The modern urethane systems are applied in a two step process called a base coat - clear coat system. The base coat, is the color(s) coat, which is then covered with a clear system which adds depth and gloss. The base coat colors are a rather dull finish, or a semi-gloss finish, and with the proper reducer, will dry to touch in about five to ten minutes. The reducer must be selected according to the temperature of the part being painted. Obviously, if you have to paint outside in bright sunlight, you may not be able to find a reducer that will work, because the surface temperature of the coach may be over 100 degrees. A bus should be painted inside a barn, a shelter or a paint booth, if possible. This will minimize the effect of the outside environment with its airborne particles, even on a calm day. After a base coat is applied, most systems will permit masking over in about thirty minutes without the tape lifting the paint. The instructions are given on each can of paint; follow them carefully.

In order to achieve a chemical bond between the base coat and the clear glossy coat, the clear coat should be applied within about 24 hours of the base coat application. The base coat will not have cured sufficiently, so that a chemical cross-linking will occur between the catalyzed clear coat and the base. This is a real problem with a very complicated graphics design, unless you have a team of talented personnel masking and painting.

A solution to this problem, if you are limited with personnel, ie., having the paint job done by only one person, is to take your time doing the base coat, assuring a perfect job. This may take days, or even weeks. Then, before applying the clear coat, scuff the entire coach with red *Scotchbright,* a plastic substitute for a scouring pad. This is somewhat like giving the coach a very fine sanding over the base coat. By doing this, a mechanical bond will be achieved, rather than a chemical bond. Will the mechanical bond be as good as the chemical bond? Probably not, but urethane has exceptional adhesive properties. Our personal coach was painted with this process six years ago, and we are still getting compliments on its new look, when I remember to wash it.

Now we must discuss a danger inherent in urethane systems. The curing agent in all urethane systems, whether they are a foam, a rubber or a coating system, is isocyanate. What is isocyanate? Isocyanate is the catalyst that allows the urethane resin to harden, or cure. In the process of use, cyanide gas is given off. The State of California uses this gas to execute convicted killers. A few years ago, Monsanto Chemical allowed, through an accident, a form of isocyanate to escape into the surrounding community of Bohpol, India, killing many people. A brief whiff of this chemical can cause permanent damage to your lungs, such as emphysema or other respiratory problems. A simple dust mask is totally inadequate to protect against this deadly gas. **A filtered respirator system is necessary with plenty of ventilation when spraying a catalyzed paint.** If you can have your coach painted inside a barn or other shelter, rent or somehow borrow enough exhaust fans to have an air change every few minutes. Your paint supplier has one-time-use disposable masks with charcoal filters to be used when applying this material.

If you plan to do your own painting, purchase a top loading paint gun. The inexpensive imported copies are very serviceable for a few-times usage, and are less than $100. The beauty of the top loading spray guns is that they have a built-in pressure regulator and can apply paint at as little as 10 psi air pressure. These types of guns have become mandatory in many areas concerned with air pollution, since over-spray is kept to a minimum. The professional painters, of course, pay a lot more for their equipment, since it must remain serviceable, for job after job.

How much should the materials cost to paint a bus? This may be generalized at approximately $1,000 to $1,500. The real answer depends on the level of complexity of your graphics, the number of colors, and the selection of colors. For example, deep reds require much more pigment, thus costing more than, say, mauve. When determining the material cost to paint a bus, all the materials must be included, such as sand paper, body filler, masking paper and tape, primer, reducer, thinner, color coat, clear coat, and catalyst. It is not uncommon to have the material cost exceed $2,500.

Most color coats will yield one and a half gallons per gallon, since the reducer is often mixed on a one-half to one basis. The clear coat should yield about two and a half gallons per gallon, since the catalyst is normally mixed on a one-to-one basis, and the reducer mixed one-half to one. How about coverage? An average forty foot bus, with the windows masked, and the lower section with bright metal not to be painted, will need about two gallons of material for each coat.

One of the advantages of this type of system is that invariably scratches will appear, as if by magic, from trees and shrubbery and other sources. But they may be buffed out if they do not penetrate the clear coat. It is easy for anyone unfamiliar with the technique to *buff* through the paint without even half trying. So take it easy! The repair may be done with 1500 or 2000 grit wet/dry sandpaper, then a fine polishing compound such as Microfinish, and finally, using a 3M product with the trade name Finesse. Use a somewhat slow polishing bonnet, so as not to overheat the surface, and it can look new in no time.

Chapter Forty Three

Engines and Transmissions

The majority of bus engines are Detroit "71" series. This engine series begun in the early "30s", and has been configured in probably more combinations than any other series engine. The designation, "71", is the size of the cylinder in cubic inches. It is a two stroke engine, meaning it fires on every up stroke and exhausts on every down stroke. As a result of this action, it has almost twice the torque rating of a four cycle engine. The most common configurations for this series of engine are the in-line-six, and the V8, although industrial applications have ranges from a 2-71 to a V12-71, and many combinations in between.

In the early 70s, the "92" series became popular for bus installation, with the V6-92 replacing the V8-71, at approximately the equivalent horsepower. In addition the newer engines became turbo-charged, although many of the V8-71s have been turbo charged. The newer V6-92 has better balance and better low end torque.

Along came air pollution concerns and then standards. The two stroke engine is definitely a dirty motor so the engineers at Detroit developed computer controlled fuel systems for the 92 series. This new system was known as the D-DEC, or Detroit Diesel Electronic Computer control system. More recently, Detroit has begun marketing their new **series 60** engines for bus and truck power. This new engine is a four cycle engine and is much cleaner burning and has a very high efficiency rating.

However, many of us with older buses and limited

budgets must be content with the older engines. Fortunately, parts and kits will continue to be made for these power plants. In addition to genuine Detroit parts, there are several after market manufacturers of parts for the older engines.

The old stand-by engine, the V8-71, is nominally rated at 318 horsepower and delivers approximately 270 horsepower to the wheels. With this motor, pulling a long tough grade tends to tax the patience of most converted bus drivers, having to be content with 25 to 30 miles per hour. So it has become popular to upgrade to the V8-92 motor. This upgrade must also include an upgrade in cooling capacity. The bigger motor produces nearly 500 horsepower and an associated increase in heat. The simple way to increase the cooling capacity is to replace your radiator with the one recommended by the factory. In some cases, the factory no longer exists, so consult with the engine manufacturer for a recommendation. In many cases, additional radiators have been added and seem to work satisfactorily.

The standard injector size for the *71* series is 60, and for the *92* series is the 90. In many cases, additional horsepower can be achieved by increasing the size of the injectors. Furthermore, even though it seems illogical, increase in fuel economy has been achieved with the larger injectors. It is common in the Northwest for logging trucks with V6-92 engines to install 105 or 110 injectors, and get not only more power, but better fuel economy. I have discussed this with Detroit representatives who have told me, "Yes, this is true, but it will shorten your engine life." So, I make no recommendation, only reporting what I have heard.

Transmissions installed in earlier buses have always been the four speed manual shift type. Many of the earlier city transit buses used a three speed automatic, but since a city transit bus is not recommended for bus conversions, this will not be discussed (I hope nobody gets their nose out of joint, sorry).

In this country the most common automatic transmission is the Allison. The Allison transmission is virtually bullet-proof. The 700 series is a heavy duty transmission and is used for semi-trucks with loads up to 80,000 pounds, and for heavy earth moving equipment. When using an V8-71 engine, the 654 Allision is a natural match. The *5* in the designated number is the number of gear ratios in the transmission. The most common automatic used against the *92* series engine is the Allison 740. This is a four speed heavy duty transmission. The reason a four speed transmission may be used on the *92* series engine is the motor has a reasonably high torque rating at low RPM. The *71* series engine does not achieve a usable torque until it reaches a high RPM , This means the RPM on the *71* must be maintained at a higher speed in order to achieve a minimum torque rating and avoid *lugging* the motor, hence the need for more gear splits.

The latest transmission to come on the scene is the B500 Allison World transmission. This transmission along with the new Detroit series 60 engines are now available in brand new bus shells from Eagle Coach Corporation.

For those of you on a limited budget, the ten speed manual transmission is a vast improvement over the old four speed box. Unless you have had trucker experience, the idea of ten speeds sounds formidable but actually they are quite simple. There are five gear locations in low range, then a splitter is actuated and the same five locations are repeated. The average ten speed transmission can be picked up at a truck salvage yard for about $800 to $1,000. More recently, a nine speed unit has become popular for around the same price range. Again, the Fuller Ten Speed Road Ranger is virtually bullet-proof when installed in a bus conversion. These units are made to work flawlessly in 80,000 pound semi-trucks, so a 35,000 pound bus conversion is an easy task.

One of the delightful features of the ten speed Road Ranger is the clutch is necessary to use only for starting, while idling at a stop or in moving away from a dead stop. After that, with a little practice, each gear may be shifted manually by synchronizing the move to the engine speed without the use of the clutch. In a way, it is almost like a poor-man's automatic. Another thing about the ten speed transmission is on a flat surface, it is common to move away from a dead stop in third gear. This leaves two lower gears to use when in an awkward position, such as being parked on a hill. The old four speed box was very unforgiving when the coach was parked facing up hill. It was necessary to rev up the engine to get up enough torque, then let out the clutch to get moving. This often fried the friction material of the clutch, thus wasting it. The author bought two new clutches before he had a ten speed transmission installed in his first coach. In an up hill condition, the ten speed transmission was simply put into first gear, often called *granny gear*, the coach would then simply crawl away from a dead stop at almost walking speed.

This chapter is designed only to give an over view. No doubt, newer and better options will be available as this goes into print.

Chapter Forty Four

Tires and Suspensions

Believe it or not, tires for big rigs are still available in tube type. This is hard to believe since we haven't had tube type tires on our cars for nearly thirty years. If you plan to do much travelling in Mexico, it is almost mandatory to use tube type tires with split rims. The tubeless tire is very difficult to locate, even in large cities such as Guadalajara. This was true, however, in 1991. By now, things may have changed. The tube type tires come in even designations such as, 10-20, or 11-22 and so forth. The tube type tires can be had as radial, which have an R designation, such as 10R20. Without the R, they are bias ply tires.

The most common tires on big rigs are the radial tubeless style. They come in various load ratings, which are an extension of the load rating of automobile tires. Most big rigs tires begin with load rating "F". This is the equivalent of a 12 ply tire. The load ratings "G" and "H" are 14 and 16 ply ratings, respectively.

The most common tire on a forty foot bus is the 12.5R22.5 size. This tire fits on a 22.5 inch diameter wheel and the equivalent load rated tire on a semi-truck is the 11R24.5 tire, which fits on a 24.5 inch diameter wheel. Truck tires are almost $100 less per tire than bus tires, since so many more trucks are on the road. If you wish to continue to employ the smaller wheel, ie., the 22.5 diameter, you may purchase the 11R22.5 truck tire in a higher load rating and still save almost $100 per tire. However, you will sacrifice a small degree of fuel economy because you are turning your motor at a specific RPM but not traveling over the ground quite as far.

If you plan to upgrade to alloy wheels for appearance, it is suggested you select the 24.5 size. You may then add the 11R24.5 tire, and the savings will help you pay for the alloy wheels. Keep in mind simply buying alloy wheels is not the only expense you will encounter. New wheel studs must be installed to accept the alloy wheels. These studs must be long enough to show about four threads after the lugs have been tightened. These longer studs, as of this writing, are about four dollars each. Multiply this times ten per wheel, times six wheels, and the added cost is over $240 plus tax, plus installation. Installation requires each brake drum be removed; have the old studs presses or beaten out and the new studs pressed in, then re-installed on the axle. Take a sample of your old stud when buying the new studs. There are many configurations of wheel studs in the catalog so don't simply tell the counterman you want a stud an inch longer. Take the old one to be sure you can compare the length and diameter of the seat.

For years, the suspension system of buses have been air bags. This was considered the standard of the industry until the Golden Eagle was introduced in 1958. The Eagle departed from convention by introducing the Torsilastic torsion bar suspension system. This is a suspension system which uses silicon rubber encased within a steel sleeve which maintains an almost uniform torsional resistance throughout its deflection range. For example, a conventional torsion bar increases the load resistance as it bends until the breaking point. Using the jacketed rubber torsion bar of the Torsilastic suspension, the load resistance is almost constant, ie., if it will resist 1 pound at 1 inch of twist, it will resist 1 pound at 2 inches of twist, and so forth. As the torsion bars tend to relax, they may be adjusted to bring back the original ground clearance. When all the adjustment has been made, the torsion bars may then be re-indexed, by removing them and rotating the mounting bolts over one bolt hole.

One of the drawbacks to the air bag suspension system is its lateral stability. In many of the older 96-inch wide coaches with air bags, they tend to lean noticeably while going around long sweeping curves, and they are visibly affected by cross winds. In the newer coaches the air bags have been placed further outboard increasing their lateral stability immensely.

In some of the older Eagles, where the torsion bars have had all their adjustment used up, air bags have been installed over them, with the added advantage of being individually inflated for leveling purposes. Many of the older coaches use a technique of valving air to individual air bags for coach leveling purposes.

The Prevosts also use their air bags for the added advantage of being able to lift their tag axle tires for tight maneuvering or when they need more load on the drive axle.

As a final point, when working on your conversion, block up your coach. Do not trust your suspension system, nor trust any jacking system you may have. Wooden blocks are cheap, and I have seen a bus fall off jacks. Fortunately, no one was under the bus when it happened.

The Bus Converter's Bible

Notes:

Sketches

Conclusions

Each coach, by each individual, is a work of art, reflecting not only their taste, but their attitude and life style. In no way, is there a wrong way to convert a coach for yourself. If you are satisfied, then its right.

The author has converted two coaches for himself and would continue to convert more if he could. Unfortunately, the physical constraints of age have reduced him to a word engineer. The author welcomes criticism of this book and will strive to incorporate any corrections and criticisms in later editions. This, of course, assumes that this edition is welcomed by those individuals purchasing this book.

The author especially welcomes comments by those in the trade, both the suppliers and converters. If any important product has been omitted through carelessness, bias, or just plain stupidity, please contact the publisher who will consider it for inclusion in the next edition.

The various tasks of converting a bus may be broken down into a number of categories. Listed below are the categories used by the author. These could, in some cases, be amalgamated, or expanded, but have traditionally been used by the author over the years of his involvement in bus conversion. If the total cost of the conversion is equal to 100 percent, then the various tasks represent a percentage of that total, as shown below.

Cost of Conversion Percentage by Category

Body (including cost and improvements). . . . 44.0
Engine & Transmission. 9.0
Plumbing 4.0
Electrical (including generator) 11.0

Heating and Air Conditioning	5.0
Cabinet work	6.0
Equipment	6.0
Instrumentation	2.0
Paint & Body work	7.0
Furnishings	6.0
Totals	100.0

A word about re-selling your conversion is now in order. You see these beautiful coaches done by Marathon, Liberty, Custom Coach and others selling for over a half-a-mil. You have done an exceptional job on your own coach, so it is natural to believe your rig, which is the size and shape of the professionally built coaches, should be valued somewhere between 100 and 200k. After you have come back to Earth, consider the following: If you discount your labor to zero, and manage to sell your coach for close to what you have in it, give yourself a ***Well Done!*** Especially considering your years of use and enjoyment.

For those of you wishing to obtain more information, you may register your purchase of this book with the publisher similar to software registration. This will make you eligible for free upgrades to specific information as it becomes available. To be more specific, this book will be revised in the future as improvements and corrections become known. These revisions will not be incorporated until the second or third printing, which may not be for a year or two. Please fill out and return the registration form in the front of this book. You will be sent the new information as it is developed at no cost, except for postage.

If you have a friend that would like a copy of this book, use one of the order blanks located in the back of the book.

GOOD LUCK AND HAPPY BUSING !!

Appendix
Quick Reference Tables

Some of the tables contained in this quick reference appendix have appeared elsewhere in the text of the book. They are repeated here so the reader doesn't have to leaf through the book looking for them. Furthermore, additional useful information is included that will aid the converter in answering those questions that commonly arise.

Amperage Capacity per Wire Size

Gage	Standard Insulation	High Temperature
14	15 amps	22 amps
12	20 amps	27 amps
10	25 amps	37 amps
8	35 amps	49 amps
6	45 amps	65 amps
4	60 amps	86 amps
2	80 amps	115 amps

Ampere Draw, Wattage per Voltage				
Wattage	12 V	24 V	120 V	240 V
100	8.4	4.2	.84	.42
200	16.7	8.4	1.7	.84
300	25	12.5	2.5	1.3
400	34	16.7	3.4	1.7
500	41.7	21	4.2	2.1
1000	84	42	8.4	4.2
1500	125	63	12.5	6.3
2000	167	84	16.7	8.4
2500	209	105	21	10.5

Screw Pullout Load in Pounds with 3/4-inch Penetration

Size	Diam.	Fir	Oak	Walnut
#6	.138	74	188	106
#7	.151	80	206	116
#8	.164	88	224	126
#10	.190	101	260	146

Strength of Steel Bolts in Tension and Shear (pounds)

Size	Area	Grade 3		Grade 5		Grade 8	
		Ten	Shear	Ten	Shear	Ten	Shear
#6	0.0123	368	245	N/A	N/A	N/A	N/A
#8	0.0191	573	382	N/A	N/A	N/A	N/A
#10	0.0275	824	549	1716	1373	N/A	N/A
1/4	.0.049	1472	981	3066	2453	4416	3680
3/8	0.077	2307	1538	4807	3845	6922	5768
3/8	0.11	3312	2208	6899	5520	9935	8279
7/16	0.137	4115	2743	8572	6858	12344	10287
1/2	0.196	5888	3925	12266	9813	17663	14716

Strength of Aluminum Alloys (psi)

Alloy	Ultimate Ten	Yield	Shear	Mod Elas
2024-0	27,000.00	11,000.00	18,000.00	10.6×10^6
2024-T3	65,000.00	45,000.00	20,000.00	10.6×10^6
6061-0	18,000.00	8,000.00	12,000.00	10.6×10^6
6061-T4	35,000.00	21,000.00	24,000.00	10.6×10^6
6061-T6	45,000.00	40,000.00	30,000.00	10.6×10^6
7075-0	33,000.00	15,000.00	17,000.00	10.4×10^6
7075-T6	76,000.00	67,000.00	46,000.00	10.4×10^6

Strength of Low Carbon (mild) Steel (psi)

AISI	Condit.	Tensile	Yield	Rockwell
1018	Hot R'd	69,000	40,000	B79
1018	Cold R'd	82,000	70,000	B85
M1020	Hot R'd	63,000	35,000	B72
1020	Hot R'd	69,000	40,000	B79
1025	T'd & Pol.	67,000	45,000	B79

Iron Pipe Size

Nominal Size	Outside Diameter	Wall Thickness Sched 40	Wall thickness Sched 80
1/8	0.405	0.068	0.095
1/4	0.54	0.088	0.119
3/8	0.675	0.091	0.126
1/2	0.84	0.109	0.147
3/4	1.05	0.113	0.154
1	1.315	0.133	0.179
1¼	1.66	0.14	0.191
1½	1.9	0.145	0.2
2	2.375	0.154	0.218
2½	2.875	0.203	0.276
3	3.5	0.216	0.3

Tap Drill Sizes

Tap Size	Std	Drill Size	Decimal
4 x 40	NC	No. 43	0.0880
6 x 32	NC	No. 36	0.1065
8 x 32	NC	No. 29	0.1360
10 x 32	NF	No. 21	0.1590
10 x 24	NC	No. 25	0.1495
12 x 24	NC	No. 16	0.1770
1/4 x 20	NC	No. 7	0.2010
1/4 x 28	NF	No. 3	0.2130
5/16 x 18	NC	17/64	0.2656
5/16 x 24	NF	17/64	0.2656
3/8 x 16	NC	5/16	0.3125
3/8 x 24	NF	21/64	0.3281
7/16 x 14	NC	3/8	0.3750
7/16 x 20	NF	25/64	0.3906
1/2 x 13	NC	27/64	0.4219
1/2 x 20	NF	29/64	0.4531

Drill Sizes for Pipe Taps

Pipe Tap Size	Drill Size	Decimal
1/8 x 27	3/8	0.3750
1/4 x 18	7/16	0.4375
1/2 x 14	3/4	0.7500
3/4 x 14	15/16	0.9375

Hard and Soft Wood Strengths (psi)

WoodType	Bending	Crushing	Shear
Hemlock	6,100	5,400	1,000
Pine	6,300	5,200	900
Ash	8,900	7,400	2,000
Birch	10,100	8,100	1,800
Cherry	9,000	7,100	1,700
Mahogany	7,900	6,800	1,200
Maple	9,500	7,300	2,300
Oak	8,200	7,400	2,000
Walnut	10,500	7,500	1,300
Doug Fir	7,800	7,400	1,100
Redwood	6,700	5,400	900

Note: The values for crushing and shear strengths are parallel to the grain

Weights of Materials

Material	Pounds/in^3	Pounds/Ft^3	Pounds/Gal
Steel	0.29 (.3)	489	N/A
Aluminum	0.096 (.1)	167	N/A
Oak	0.028	48	N/A
Doug Fir	0.018	32	N/A
Water	0.036	62.4	8.35
Diesel Fuel	0.032	55	7.35
Gasoline	0.026	46	6.15

USEFUL INFORMATION

To find circumference of a circle, multiply diameter by 3.1416.
To find diameter of a circle, multiply circumference by .31831.
To find area of a circle, multiply square of diameter by .7854.
Area of a rectangle = length multiplied by breadth.
Doubling the diameter of a circle increases its area four times.
To find area of a triangle, multiply base by ½ perpendicular height.
Area of ellipse = product of both diameters x .7854.
Area of a parallelogram = base x altitude.
To find cubic inches in a ball, multiply cube of diameter by .5236.
To find cubic contents of a cone, multiply area of base by ⅓ the altitude.

Surface of frustrum of cone or pyramid = sum of circumference of both ends x ½ slant height, plus area of both ends.

Contents of frustrum of cone or pyramid = multiply area of two ends and get square root. Add the 2 areas and x ⅓ altitude.

Doubling the diameter of a pipe increases its capacity four times.

A gallon of water (U. S. standard) weighs 8.35 lbs. and contains 231 cubic inches.

A cubic foot of water contains 7½ gallons, 1728 cubic inches. and weighs 62.4 lbs.

To find the pressure in pounds per square inch of a column of water. multiply the height of the column in feet by .434.

Steam rising from water at its boiling point (212 F.) has a pressure equal to the atmosphere (14.7 lbs. to the square inch.)

A standard horse power: the evaporation of 30 lbs. of water per hour from a feed water temperature of 100 F. into steam at 70 lbs. gauge pressure.

A standard horsepower: 550 ft-lbs per sec.(33,000 ft-lbs per min.), or 746 watts

To find capacity of a tank any size, given dimensions of a cylinder in inches: to find its capacity in U. S. gallons: square the diameter, multiply by the length and by .0034.

For every ten degrees of temperature increase, a bar of aluminum 1000 inches (83.33 ft.) long will grow 1/8 of an inch, and the same length of steel will grow 1/16th of an inch..

Appendix

Insulation Comparisons

Material	R value/inch thickness	cost per inch per sq ft	Cost/R value
Rockwool	3	5 cents	1.6 cents
Urethane Foam	7	38 cents	5.4 cents
Fiberglass	3	6 cents	2.0 cents
(superinsulation)	25	5.00 dollars	20.0 cents
bubble foil	7	48 cents	6.8 cents

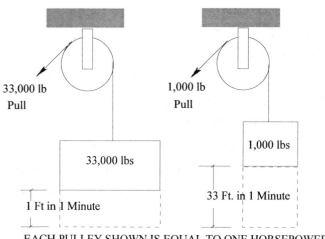

ILLUSTRATION OF HORSEPOWER

33,000 lb Pull — 33,000 lbs — 1 Ft in 1 Minute

1,000 lb Pull — 1,000 lbs — 33 Ft. in 1 Minute

EACH PULLEY SHOWN IS EQUAL TO ONE HORSEPOWER

Torque (T) is the product of Force (W) x radius (R) in inches from the center of a shaft in inch-lbs

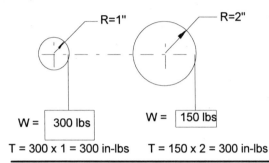

T = 300 x 1 = 300 in-lbs   T = 150 x 2 = 300 in-lbs

If the shaft is rotated the force (W) is moved through a distance, and Work is done

$$\text{Work (ft-lbs)} = W \times \frac{2\pi R}{12} \times \text{No of Rev of Shaft}$$

When this Work is done in a specified Time, Power is used

$$\text{Power (ft-lbs per min.)} = W \times \frac{2\pi R}{12} \times RPM$$

Since 1 Horsepower = 33,000 ft-lbs per minute

$$HP = W \times \frac{2\pi R}{12} \times \frac{RPM}{33,000} = \frac{W \times R \times RPM}{63,025}$$

Since Torque (in-lbs) = Force (W) x Radius (R), Therefore

$$HP = \frac{\text{Torque (T)} \times RPM}{63,025}$$

Index

Air bags 264
Airconditioning 157, 201-216
Allison 261
AlumaCool 196
Amperage 126, 269
AquaHot 185
Awnings 198
Baggage compartment 43
Base coat 255
Battery 119
Battery charger 129
Bellmouth 60
Bending stress 271
Black water 97
Blinds 233
Body work 245
Boiler 180
Bondo 245
Box beam 40
Breaker 143
BTU 165
Bulkheads 225
Bumper jack 26
Bus Conversion magazine 13
Cabinets 237
CAD 219
Central air conditioning 205
Carpet 241
Catalytic heater 189
Circuit 139

Clear coat	255
Coleman	205
Compression stress	31
Computer Aided Design	219
Conduction	168
Convection	169
Converter	129
Coolant	183
Corian	237
Detroit	259
Diesel heater	180
Dometic	188
DOT	23
Doublers	37
Drapes	233
Duct work	207
Eagle	12,13,31,35,59
Electric heater	186
Electrical Systems	113
Electronic	149
Engines	259
Fantastic vent	196
Fiberglass	245
Fittings	103
Fixtures	89
Floor	241
Floor plans	219
Flooring	241
Flxible	13
Fresh water	77
Fuller Road Ranger	261
Gauges	153

Index

Generator	123
GM 4104	13, 15
GM 4106	13
GPS	156
Graphics	253
Grey water	99
Headliners	229
Heating	179-194
Hinge	238
Horsepower	277
Instrumentation	153
Insulation	163
Interior design	217
Inverter	129
Isocyanate	256
Jack	26
Koolamatic	196
L P G	107
Main panel	141, 142
Maintainability	59
Masking paper	249
MCI	13
Modulus of elasticity	52
Mullion	25
National Bus Trader magazine	13
Ozite	230
Paint	253
Panel	143
Perfect-Toe heater	186
Photovoltaic cell	131
Pipe	103
Platinum Cat	189

Plumbing	69
Power panel	143
Prime coat	249
Primus	187
ProHeat	184
Propane heater	187
Pump	72, 85
R-factor	165
Radiation	170
Radiator	59
Refrigerants	203
Relay	141
Roof air conditioning	208
Roof raising	23
Roof frame	36
Screw pull-out loads	270
Shades	233
Siding	51
Skin	51
Slide-out	37
Sliding window	233
Solar panel	132
Solid wire	133
Split air conditioning	206
Steel	272
Stranded wire	135
Stress	31
Sub panel	141
Tanks	77, 96, 107
Tape	249
Thermal conductivity	165
Thermostat	187, 203

Index

Tires 263
Torsion bars 264
Torsional stress 65
Transmission 261
Truss 30
Urethane 255
Ventilation 195
Vinyl 229
Voltage 270
Walls 225
Waste water 95
Wattage 270
Webasto 181
Window 233
Wiring 269

The Bus Converter's Bible

Order Form

The Bus Converter's Bible

Name _____

Address _____

City _____ State _____ Zip _____

Phone Number (_____) _____

If you would like an additional copy of this book for you or your friends, please fill out this form and mail to:

    WINLOCK publishing company
    26135 Murrieta Road
    Sun City, CA 92585
    or
    Phone (909)943-4945

Number of Copies: _____ @ $ 49.95 _____

    Shipping $ 5.00 _____

Please add 7 ¾ percent sales tax _____
for California residents
        Total _____

I understand that I may return this book for a full refund, for any reason, no questions asked.

Order Form

The Bus Converter's Bible

Name _____

Address _____

City _____ State _____ Zip _____

Phone Number (_____) _____

If you would like an additional copy of this book for you or your friends, please fill out this form and mail to:

> *WINLOCK publishing company*
> *26135 Murrieta Road*
> *Sun City, CA 92585*
> *or*
> *Phone (909)943-4945*

Number of Copies: _____ @ $ 49.95 _____

    Shipping $ 5.00   _____

Please add 7 ¾ percent sales tax   _____
for California residents
                Total   _____

I understand that I may return this book for a full refund, for any reason, no questions asked.